Legal Guide for Police

Constitutional Issues

Second Edition

John C. Klotter, J.D.
Professor Emeritus and Former Dean
School of Justice Administration
University of Louisville

anderson publishing co.
2035 reading road
cincinnati, ohio 45202
(513) 421-4142

Legal Guide for Police, Constitutional Issues, Second Edition

ISBN 0-87084-498-9
Library of Congress Catalog Number 89-83248

Kelly Humble *Managing Editor*

PREFACE

Today, law enforcement officials must be highly skilled in the use of investigative tools and extremely knowledgeable in the intricacies of the law. One error in judgment during the initial contact with the violator could, and often does, impede the investigation. For example, an illegal search or unauthorized questioning may so contaminate the evidence that it will be forever useless for investigative or prosecution purposes. Such errors often result in the liberation of dangerous criminals.

In addition to the loss of use of evidence for prosecution purposes, failure to comply with the constitutional mandates often leads to personal liability on the part of the officer, administrator or the agency. However, a knowledge of the Constitution as interpreted by the courts can avoid unauthorized action and make it possible for the officer to act with more confidence.

The legal rules under which a law enforcement officer must operate as a trained professional are not simple, but neither are they impossible to master. The trend toward uniformity in state and federal laws in the area of criminal justice makes it possible to enunciate general standards which may be applicable in all jurisdictions. However, a state, by statute or by interpretation of its own constitution, may place additional restrictions on the use of evidence. It is, therefore, necessary that the police officer, especially the investigator, and the administrator be familiar with both federal and state laws and decisions interpreting the state constitutional provisions.

Due to the "federalization of the Bill of Rights," most of the protections of the first eight amendments which originally restricted only the federal agents now are applicable to the states by way of the Fourteenth Amendment. The United States Supreme Court, using the Fourteenth Amendment as the conduit, has now established minimum standards which must be followed by all public enforcement officials.

After discussing the effects of failure to comply with constitutional mandates and considering the general limitations on police power, emphasis is placed on the common constitutional questions that confront the officer when he is called on to enforce the law. In particular, the legal standards relating to detention, arrest, search, questioning suspects and pre-trial identification procedures are stated and discussed.

This book is designed for the officer who has the important task of protecting, seeking and preparing evidence for use in court. It may be used in departmental training programs as well as in junior colleges that offer courses for in-service and pre-service officers. For a more comprehensive discussion of constitutional law as it relates to criminal justice practice, reference is made to Klotter and Kanovitz, *Constitutional Law*, 5th Edition, Anderson Publishing Co., 1985 with the 1987 supplement.

Because the law in this area is constantly changing, it is necessary for all criminal justice personnel to keep up to date by reading United States Supreme Court decisions. Also, from time to time the author will prepare a supplement or update the material.

John C. Klotter

Table of Contents

Preface   *iii*

Chapter 1   1
Results of Failure to Comply
with Constitutional Mandates

§1.1   Civil liabilities   2
§1.2   Civil rights actions   2
§1.3   Liability of supervisors, administrators and agencies   6
§1.4   Admissibility of evidence   9
§1.5   Summary   11

Chapter 2   13
Police Power and Limitations

§2.1   Police responsibility   14
§2.2   Limits on police authority   14
§2.3   Bill of Rights   15
§2.4   Due process of law   16
§2.5   Effects of broadening the scope of the   17
       Fourteenth Amendment due process clause
§2.6   Protection of rights via state constitutions and laws   17
§2.7   Summary   18

Chapter 3   21
Police Authority to Detain

§3.1	General considerations	22
§3.2	Legislation concerning the authority to detain	22
§3.3	*Terry v. Ohio* stop and frisk rationale	25
§3.4	Application to off-street situations	27
§3.5	Application to detention of motorists	28
§3.6	Detention of luggage	29
§3.7	Duration of the detention	31
§3.8	Detention to check driver's license and registration	31
§3.9	Summary	32

Chapter 4   35
Law of Arrest

§4.1	General considerations	36
§4.2	Statutory authority to arrest	37
§4.3	Definition and elements of arrest	39
§4.4	Arrest under authority of an arrest warrant	42
§4.5	Arrest without a warrant	51
§4.6	Use of force in making an arrest	61
§4.7	The citation and summons in law enforcement	63
§4.8	Arrest after fresh pursuit	65
§4.9	Summary	66

Chapter 5   69
Search and Seizure with a Warrant

§5.1	General considerations	70
§5.2	Constitutional provisions	71
§5.3	The exclusionary rule	71
§5.4	Extension of the exclusionary rule to all courts: *Mapp v. Ohio*	72
§5.5	Application and modification of the exclusionary rule	73
§5.6	Seizure with a valid search warrant – general	76
§5.7	Requirements of a valid search warrant	77
§5.8	Execution of the search warrant	84
§5.9	Search of a person on the premises where such person is not described in the warrant	87
§5.10	Return of the warrant	89
§5.11	Advantage of the search under a valid warrant	89
§5.12	Summary	90

Chapter 6   **93**
Search and Seizure without a Warrant

§6.1	General considerations	95
§6.2	Search incidental to a lawful arrest	95
§6.3	Search with a valid waiver	103
§6.4	Search of movable vehicles and objects	107
§6.5	Seizure without a search (plain view)	110
§6.6	Search by a private individual	112
§6.7	Search of premises not protected by the Fourth Amendment (open fields)	114
§6.8	Standing to challenge the search	116
§6.9	Search after lawful impoundment – inventory searches	118
§6.10	Stop and frisk seizures	120
§6.11	Search of pervasively regulated business	124
§6.12	Seizure of verbal evidence via concealed recorders or microphones	125
§6.13	Summary	127

Chapter 7   **129**
Questioning Suspects

§7.1	General considerations	131
§7.2	The free and voluntary rule	131
§7.3	The delay in arraignment rule	133
§7.4	Warning and waiver requirements (*Miranda* rule)	134
§7.5	Exclusion of confession as a means of enforcing the Fourth Amendment	143
§7.6	Right to counsel	144
§7.7	Corroboration	147
§7.8	Derivative evidence	148
§7.9	Admissible statements (including "Good Faith" exception)	148
§7.10	Admissibility of a second confession after an inadmissible first confession	151
§7.11	Summary	152

Chapter 8
Pre-Trial Identification Procedures   **155**

§8.1	General considerations	156
§8.2	Fingerprinting and photographing suspects	156
§8.3	Lineup – self-incrimination challenge	157
§8.4	Lineup – right to counsel challenge	158
§8.5	Lineup – due process challenge	159
§8.6	Pre-trial photographic identification	161
§8.7	Dental examination	162
§8.8	Voice exemplars	162
§8.9	Footprint comparisons and other body examinations	163
§8.10	Summary	163

Appendix   **165**
**Bill of Rights (First Ten Amendments)
and Fourteenth Amendment**

Index   **169**

Chapter 1

RESULTS OF FAILURE TO COMPLY WITH CONSTITUTIONAL MANDATES

The question in this case is whether a reasonably well-trained officer in petitioner's position would have known that his affidavit failed to establish probable cause and that he should not have applied for the warrant.

Malley v. Briggs, 106 S.Ct. 1092 (1986)
(Civil Rights action against trooper
alleging unconstitutional arrest)

Section
1.1   Civil liabilities
1.2   Civil rights actions
1.3   Liability of supervisors, administrators and agencies
1.4   Admissibility of evidence
1.5   Summary

Failure to comply with the mandates of the United States Constitution as interpreted by the courts results not only in the loss of cases but in liability on the part of the officer as well as the administrator and the agency. Failure on the part of the agency to properly train or to enact and enforce guidelines which are consistent with the constitutional provisions often results in civil actions in state courts as well as actions in federal courts under the civil rights statutes. In this chapter the discussion relates to areas of possible liability for failure to abide by constitutional mandates. In the chapters which follow, these constitutional requirements are discussed in detail.

§1.1   Civil liabilities

When civil action is initiated against a police officer or an administrator, it is generally under the tort law that applies in the jurisdiction where the action is brought. If the tort action is instigated by the plaintiff, he must prove that (1) a duty existed on the part of the defendant, (2) the defendant breached that duty, (3) there was a causal connection between the breach of the duty and the injury, and (4) the injuries to the plaintiff resulted from that breach.

When determining if a duty does in fact exist, the court looks to the Constitution of the United States, the constitutions of the various states, statutes, ordinances, departmental regulations, and cases decided by the courts. If a violation of a constitutional mandate, such as a violation of the Fourth Amendment, is proved, this can serve as a basis for civil action in state court. For example, if an arrest violates the constitutional provision, as interpreted by the Supreme Court, that arrest may serve as a basis for a state tort action as well as a federal action under the civil rights statutes.

More actions are initiated in civil court against police and administrators than in criminal court as it is less difficult to prove that a duty has been breached and the plaintiff is more likely to obtain civil judgment. The reasons are that in a civil tort action the plaintiff is only required to show a breach of duty by the *preponderance* of the evidence rather than beyond a reasonable doubt. Also, in a tort action, as distinguished from a criminal action, judgment may be rendered on less than a unanimous jury decision.

§1.2   Civil rights actions

a.   Civil actions

Although the civil rights statutes under which most actions are initiated against police for failure to comply with constitutional mandates were passed just after the civil war, only recently have they been utilized extensively. The

Civil Rights Statute which provides civil remedies for official misconduct was enacted by Congress in 1871 and now is codified under Title 42 of U.S. Code Section 1983.

This statute provides:

> Every person who, under color of any statute, ordinance, regulation, custom, or usage, of any state or territory, subjects, causes, or causes to be subjected, any citizen of the United States or other person within the jurisdiction thereof, to the deprivation of any rights, privileges, or immunities secured by the Constitution and laws, shall be liable to the party injured in an action at law, suit in equity, or other proper proceeding for redress.

CIVIL RIGHTS ACTIONS
Failure to Follow Constitutional Mandates

STATUTE	TYPE ACTION	KEY ELEMENTS	DEFENSES
42 USC Sec. 1983	CIVIL	1. Under Color of Law 2. Deprivation of Constitutional Rights	(1) Reasonable Good Faith
18 USC Sec. 242	CRIMINAL	1. Under Color of Law 2. Deprivation of Const. Rights 3. Specific Intent	(2) No Specific Intent

(1) Based on knowledge of Constitutional law
(2) No specific intent to deprive person of Constitutional right

In order to successfully pursue an action in federal court under Section 1983, the person who claims an injury must establish that the defendant against whom the action is brought acted "under color of statute, ordinance, regulation, custom, or usage" and that the defendant deprived the injured party of "rights, privileges, or immunities" secured by the Constitution or laws of the United States. Most police officers act under color of law in carrying out their responsibilities. The primary concern of the plaintiff is to show that by his actions the officer deprived him of a constitutional right as made clear by the constitution or decision. Once a decision is made and the constitutional right has been determined, the police are presumed to know that such rights exist. This makes it mandatory that police and administrators not only be familiar with the constitutional rights as interpreted but keep up-to-date as new decisions are rendered by the Supreme Court.

If action is instigated against a police officer under Section 1983, one of the defenses is known as the "good faith" defense or "good faith immunity." The courts have emphasized, however, that good faith alone will not be a defense under Section 1983. To prevail, the officer must prove (1) that he believed in good faith that his conduct was lawful, and (2) that such belief was reasonable under an objective standard. Once the law has been crystallized and made certain, one claiming defense of good faith based on ignorance has little claim to judicial sympathy.

In 1986 in the case of *Malley v. Briggs*, the United States Supreme Court reiterated that a police officer is not entitled to absolute immunity from liability under Section 1983 but only to qualified immunity.[1] In the *Briggs* case, a state trooper prepared felony complaints charging the defendant with possession of marijuana. The judge signed the warrants and the suspects were arrested, but the charges were subsequently dropped when the grand jury did not return an indictment. The plaintiff in the action against the officer alleged that the officer, in applying for the arrest warrants, violated his rights under the Fourth and Fourteenth Amendments. The officer claimed he acted in good faith believing that the facts in the affidavit were true. In holding the officer liable even though he relied on a judicial officer's judgment in issuing the warrant, the Supreme Court held that:

> The question is whether a reasonably *well trained* officer in petitioner's position should have known that the affidavit failed to establish probable cause. (emphasis added)

This case reaffirmed past decisions which determined that the police officer has a responsibility to be familiar with the constitutional requirements and the administrator has the responsibility of providing essential information to the officer.

---

[1]   *Malley v. Briggs*, L.Ed.2 __U.S.__, 106 S.Ct. 1093 (1986).

b.   Criminal action

Failure to comply with the constitutional mandates as interpreted by the courts also may result in criminal action against the officer in federal court. The federal law which defines the criminal violation was enacted in 1886 and is now codified as Title 18, U.S. Code Section 242. This provides that:

> Whoever, under color of any law, statute, ordinance, regulation, or custom, willfully subjects any inhabitants of any state, territory, or district, to the deprivation of any rights, privileges, or immunities secured or protected by the constitution or laws of the United States, or to different punishments, pains, or penalties, on account of such inhabitant being an alien, or by reason of his color or race, than are prescribed for the punishment of citizens, shall be fined not more than $1,000 or imprisoned not more than one year, or both; and if death results shall be subject to imprisonment for any term of years or life.

Title 18, Section 242 requires that the federal prosecutor introduce evidence to show that the person charged was acting under color of law, that there was a deprivation of rights protected by the Constitution or laws of the United States, and that the defendant acted willfully or intentionally to deprive a person of the rights protected. The first two requirements are similar to those required when action is in civil court under Title 42, Section 1983, however, a third requirement is added which mandates that the prosecution show that the officer who acted under color of law did so willfully or intentionally.

While it is more difficult to prove a criminal case under Section 242 than to successfully pursue civil action under Section 1983, there is no doubt that a police officer acting in the scope of his employment who deprives a person of a constitutional right as made certain by the court may be prosecuted in federal court.

The two elements that are common to both civil actions under Section 1983 and criminal action under Section 242 are "acting under color of law," and "deprivation of a constitutional right." Where action is under Section 1983, the plaintiff, through his attorney, must show that this deprivation occurred. When criminal action is under Section 242, the federal prosecutor must demonstrate that the officer deprived a person of a constitutional right. As was noted, when action is under Section 1983 reasonable good faith is a defense. Under Section 242, a defense of an officer who is charged is that he did not act "willfully" as required by the statute.[2] This defense, however, is of no avail if the officer acted through ignorance of the rights protected by the Constitution. If an officer knowingly or unknowingly willfully deprives a person of a right which is protected by one of the specific provisions of the Constitution, he may be liable under Section 242 as well as Section 1983. Also, once a due process right has been defined and made specific by a court decision, that right is encompassed by Section 242 of the Civil Rights Statute.[3]

§1.3   Liability of supervisors, administrators and agencies

Not only is the officer who deprives a person of a constitutional right often liable for failure to protect those rights, but the supervisor, administrator or agency may be held liable under a theory which is often referred to as "vicarious liability." While some government agencies, especially state agencies, are still not liable due to the doctrine of sovereign immunity, this doctrine has been rejected in many states by statute or court decisions.

Some courts have applied the "respondeat superior" legal principle and have held agencies liable for the acts of the officers who deprive a person of a right protected by the state or federal constitution, the laws of the states, the ordinances of political subdivisions, departmental regulations, or court decisions.

Under this principle, the master is liable for the acts of his servant where the tortious conduct of the employee is so closely connected in time, place, and causation that it is regarded as a risk of harm fairly attributable to the employer or business. For example, in the case of *Lamkin v. Brooks*, the Supreme Court of Louisiana decided that tortious conduct of the police officer toward an individual outside of the geographical limits of the town was such as to render the town vicariously liable under the theory of respondeat superior when the officer was acting within the scope of his employment.[4] In this case the officer, acting in the scope of his employment, was accused of striking the plaintiff on the head without just cause while investigating a traffic violation and intoxication offense.

---

[2] *Screws v. United States*, 325 U.S. 91, 65 S.Ct. 1031 (1945).
[3] *United States v. Stokes*, 506 F. 2d 771 (1975).
[4] *Lamkin v. Brooks*, 498 So. 2d 1068 (La. 1986).

a. Vicarious liability under Section
42 U.S. Code, Section 1983

The United States Supreme Court in earlier cases determined that police agencies were not persons under Section 1983 and were therefore not liable where officers of the agency deprived persons of their constitutional rights.   However, in 1978 that Court made it quite clear that local government officials, sued in their official capacity, are "persons" under Section 1983 and may be held liable for constitutional deprivations made pursuant to government customs even though some customs have not received formal approval through the government's official decision-making channels.[5]

The court explained in the *Monell* case that the language of Section 1983 compelled the conclusion that Congress did not intend a local government to be held liable solely because it employs a tortfeasor.   That is, it cannot be held liable under the respondeat superior theory.   However, local governing bodies and local officials may be sued directly under Section 1983 for monetary, declaratory, and injunctive relief in those situations where the action that is alleged to be unconstitutional implements or executes a policy statement, ordinance, regulation or decision officially adopted or promulgated by those whose edicts or acts may fairly be said to represent official policy.

Under this interpretation, the acts of the chief of police and his subordinates in their official capacity, whether "de jure" or "de facto," equate with the acts of this city itself.[6]   In the *Spell* case the action was brought against the patrolman, the city, the command sergeant, director of the internal affairs division, the chief of police and the city manager for injury received by an arrestee.   The court decided that the evidence supported a finding that the patrolman did assault a drug felon during and after the arrest and that the assault proximately resulted from a *de facto* policy developed by supervisory officials.

While it is clear that written policy established by an explicit directive will make a city liable for the acts of the employees of the department, official policy also may be established by a *de facto* policy.   The burden is on the plaintiff in a civil rights action to show that the *de facto* policy did, in fact, exist.   This becomes difficult in some instances, but the Supreme Court shed some light on this requirement in two cases decided in 1985 and 1986.

In the case of *City of Oklahoma v. Tuttle* in 1985 the Supreme Court held that it was reversible error to allow the jury to infer a policy of inadequate

---

[5] *Monell v. Department of Social Services of the City of New York*, 436 U.S. 658, 56 L.Ed.2d 11, 98 S.Ct. 2018 (1978).

[6] *Spell v. McDaniel*, 604 F. Supp. 641 (1985).

training on the city's part for a single shooting incident thereby giving rise to liability under Title 42, Section 1983.[7] Here the court indicated that a *de facto* policy cannot be established by one act of an officer who is not acting in an official decision-making capacity. The court explained that there must be an affirmative link between the municipality's policy and the particular constitutional violation which was alleged. If a policy of inadequate training on the part of the city is to be the basis of an action, there must be a pattern established or some substantial proof the policy was established or acquiesced in by a municipal policy maker.

One year later, the Supreme Court decided that municipal liability may be imposed for a single decision if the decision is made by a municipal policymaker responsible for establishing final policy.[8] The court reasoned that this case differed from the Oklahoma City case in that here the instructions to "go in and get the employees" came from a county prosecutor who under Ohio law was authorized to give instructions to the county sheriff. The county prosecutor was acting as the final decision maker for the county, and the county may therefore be held liable under Section 1983.

These cases make it clear that an agency or policymaker may be liable for acts of subordinates if a *de facto* or *de jure* policy has been established.

b.   Theories for attaching liability

Plaintiffs who initiate action against police officers for depriving them of constitutional rights often join the supervisors, administrators, and agencies in order to reach those who have the "deepest pocket." Also, it can be assumed that the plaintiff will predicate action on as many theories of wrongdoing as he can. For example, action may be brought for failure to properly investigate personnel before appointment, failure to properly train, failure to supervise and control, failure to discipline, or failure to terminate officers who have proved unfit for carrying out their duties. For purpose of this work, the emphasis is placed on the necessity of training officers, especially regarding the constitutional mandates.

The courts have recognized that municipalities and police administrators have an affirmative duty to train police officers whom they employ. Breach of that duty which proximately causes the injury to the plaintiff can result in personal liability on the part of the administrator or liability on the part of the agency. Courts have been particularly willing to find liability for failure to train where the use of firearms is involved.

---

[7] See *Oklahoma City v. Tuttle*, L.Ed. (2d) __ U.S.__, 105 S.Ct. 2427 (1985).

[8] *Pembaur v. City of Cincinnati*, L.Ed. (2d) __ U.S.__, __ L.Ed.2d, 106 S.Ct. 1292 (1986).

Failure to adequately train officers regarding constitutional protections could result in liability on the part of the administrator and the agency as well as the individual officer. For example, in the case of *Burquist v. County of Cochise*, the complaint alleged a causal connection between the policy of inadequate training in search and seizure procedures and the resulting injury to the plaintiffs.[9] The plaintiffs alleged that the officers who obtained the warrant did not have proper training concerning probable cause nor did they have proper training relating to the execution of the warrant. In fact, the officers had executed the warrant at the wrong house and had caused considerable damage to equipment and art works during the execution. The court, citing other cases, determined that there is little question that a policy of inadequate training can result in agency liability. If there is an official condoning or authorizing of unconstitutional acts, and the plaintiffs can demonstrate an affirmative link between the failure to train and the misconduct, then the policy of gross negligence in training and supervision gives rise to Section 1983 liability.

It is mandatory that officers and administrators be aware of the constitutional rights. As one court stated, an act violating constitutional rights can no more be justified by ignorance or disregard of settled, indisputable law...than by the presence of actual malice. The responsibility for knowing the constitutional mandates must be shared by the officer and the administrator. Not only must the officer have a reasonable understanding of these rights, but the knowledge must be updated on a continuing basis.

§1.4   Admissibility of evidence

Perhaps the most costly result of failure to comply with constitutional mandates is that the evidence will be inadmissible and a person guilty of serious crimes will go free.

a. Search and seizure exclusionary rule

This will be discussed in the chapter on search and seizure. With some exceptions, evidence obtained by search and seizure which violates the Fourth Amendment standards as interpreted by the Supreme Court is not admissible in criminal cases. This search and seizure exclusionary rule was first established in the case of *Weeks v. United States* in 1914.[10] At the time the rule was established by the Supreme Court, it applied only to federal offi-

---

[9] *Burquist v. Cochise*, 806 F. 2d 1364 (9th Cir. 1986).
[10] *Weeks v. United States*, 232 U.S. 383, 58 L.Ed. 652, 34 S.Ct. 341 (1914).

cers. However, in 1961 the Supreme Court reversed previous cases and clearly stated that the exclusionary rule which relates to search and seizure henceforth would be applied in both federal and state courts.[11] A result of this search and seizure exclusionary rule is that, in most instances, if evidence is obtained by an illegal search, it will not be admissible. Evidence so contaminated by the illegal search cannot be decontaminated and cannot be used at the trial against the defendant. There are some exceptions to the rule, such as the "good faith" exception which will be discussed in future chapters.

b. Inadmissibility of "confession" evidence

The free and voluntary rule which prohibits the use of confessions obtained by force or duress has been in effect throughout the country since it was founded. The confession exclusionary rule has been broadened so that most evidence obtained without the administration of the *Miranda* warnings is not admissible, nor is evidence admissible if there is an unnecessary delay in bringing the person arrested before a judicial officer. Exceptions to these rules are discussed in the chapter relating to questioning suspects.

c. The right to counsel exclusionary rule

In discussing the Right to Counsel Exclusionary Rule, the court in the case of *Nix v. Williams* noted that the rationale for the rule is that the fruit of unlawful police conduct is excluded because such a course is needed to deter police from violation of constitutional and statutory protections. Under this rule, some evidence obtained as a result of failure to comply with the Sixth Amendment Right to Counsel is excluded, notwithstanding "the high social cost of letting obviously guilty persons go unpunished."[12]

Failure to comply with the constitutional provisions concerning right to counsel as interpreted by the courts does not always make the evidence inadmissible. It is mandatory that officers, especially investigators, be aware of those situations when the right to counsel exclusionary rule does not apply.

---

[11] *Mapp v. Ghio*, 367 U.S. 643, 6 L.Ed. 2d 1081, 81 S.Ct. 1648 (1961).
[12] *Nix v. Williams*, 467 U.S. 431, 81 L.Ed.2d 377, 104 S.Ct. 2501 (1984).

§1.5   Summary

Before studying the specific provisions of the constitution which limit police activity, it is important to understand the effects of failure to comply with the constitutional mandates as interpreted by the courts.

An officer, on assuming the responsibilities of his office, takes an oath to support the Constitution of the United States. In most instances, however, he is unaware of the specific provisions of the Constitution and not acquainted with the fact that liabilities can result from this lack of knowledge.

A police officer is subject to civil liability under the state tort laws if he fails to comply with the constitutional provisions, state laws, ordinances, or decisions.

In addition to liability under the state tort laws, civil action may be brought in federal court under Title 42, Section 1983. Under this title, the officer is liable if he acts under color of law and deprives a person of a constitutional right. The officer may also be liable criminally under Title 18, Section 242 for failure to comply with the constitutional mandates and acting with willful intent.

Supervisors and administrators cannot escape liability even if they do not take an active part in the violation of a constitutional right. Under the respondeat superior doctrine established at common law, agencies may be liable for the acts of the employees when the employees are acting in the scope of their employment. If the administrator or supervisor fails to properly train or supervise the employee, he, as well as the agency he represents, may be subject to liability.

In addition to possible liability for failure to comply with constitutional mandates, in many instances evidence obtained in violation of these provisions is excluded. As a result, valid and pertinent evidence is not admitted even though this would help in determining the facts of the case and even though a person who is obviously guilty might go free.

While a study of the constitutional mandates will not guarantee that civil action will not be brought against the officer or administrator or that evidence will always be admissible, there is no doubt that a thorough knowledge of the most important constitutional provisions will drastically reduce the number of civil and criminal actions and will result in more evidence being admitted at the trial.

Chapter 2

POLICE POWER AND LIMITATIONS

Due process of law is a summarized constitutional guarantee of respect for those personal immunities which are "so rooted in the traditions and conscience of our people as to be ranked as fundamental" or are "implicit in the concept of ordered liberty."

Rochin v. California, 342 U.S. 165,
96 L.Ed.2d 183, 72 S.Ct. 205 (1952)

Section
2.1   Police responsibility
2.2   Limits on police authority
2.3   Bill of Rights
2.4   Due process of law
2.5   Effects of broadening the scope of the
        Fourteenth Amendment due process clause
2.6   Protection of rights via state constitutions and laws
2.7   Summary

13

§2.1   Police responsibility

As a condition to employment, law enforcement officers are required to take an oath to enforce state and federal laws and often city ordinances. In carrying out the responsibilities as designated by state statute, city ordinance, or departmental rules and regulations, the officer must often detain, arrest, search, or question a suspect. Because of the peculiar position in which the officer is placed, he has much more legal authority than the average citizen. But more importantly, he has the responsibility to use that authority with prudence and discretion.

| INDIVIDUAL | PROTECTION |
| RIGHTS | OF SOCIETY |

§2.2   Limits on police authority

Although sworn law enforcement officials have greater powers than the average citizen, these powers are not without limits. Article VI of the Constitution of the United States makes it mandatory that all executive and judicial officers, both of the United States and of the several states, shall be bound by oath or affirmation to support the Constitution of the United States. If in carrying out the police powers of the state there is conflict between the enforcement of the statutory laws and protection of the constitutional rights as interpreted by the Supreme Court, the former must give way. For example, the Supreme Court has determined that only certain searches are reasonable under the Constitution. If, in enforcing a state law, the officer makes an unreasonable search, the protections, as guaranteed by the Constitution, will be given priority.

§2.3   Bill of Rights

When the Constitution of the United States was ratified and became effective in 1789, the Federal Constitution had no Bill of Rights. Those who opposed a Bill of Rights argued that such a guarantee was unnecessary inasmuch as the powers granted to Congress were expressed powers and that limiting language was unnecessary. However, most of the states that finally ratified the Constitution submitted amendments to the Constitution to be acted on after the new government became operative.

At the first session of Congress, ten amendments to the Constitution were approved and later ratified by three-fourths of the states. These first ten amendments are known as the Bill of Rights.[1] The Bill of Rights was not intended to establish any novel principles of government but only to embody certain guarantees and immunities which the colonies had inherited from their English ancestors and which had from time immemorial been subject to certain well-recognized exceptions arising from the necessities of the case. The Bill of Rights, when adopted, was intended to apply only to the national government. As such, the amendments did not restrict the respective states in any way.

The provisions of the Bill of Rights establish the foundation for statutes and court decisions concerning search and seizure, arrest, questioning procedures, the right to counsel and other restrictions which limit action by public officials. Those of primary concern to law enforcement personnel are summarized here and discussed in detail in future chapters.

The Fourth Amendment prohibits unreasonable search and seizure of persons or property.

The Fifth Amendment enumerates safeguards for persons accused of a crime. It provides, among other things, that no person shall be compelled in any criminal case to be a witness against himself and no person shall be deprived of life, liberty, or property without due process of law.

---

[1]   Reference is made to the appendix for the specific wording of the first ten amendments.

The Sixth Amendment assures that in criminal prosecutions the accused shall enjoy the right to a speedy and public trial by an impartial jury, the right to be confronted by witnesses against him, and the right to have the assistance of counsel for his defense.

These three amendments are of primary concern to justice personnel but they would mean little without court interpretation. The facts of each individual case must be examined to determine the restrictions placed upon those charged with enforcing the law.

§2.4   Due process of law

As was noted, the Fifth Amendment when ratified in 1791 included a provision that: "No person shall be deprived of life, liberty, or property, without due process of law...."

This provision was adopted because some who had just thrown off the yoke of a tyrannical sovereign feared a strong central government.

It was not until 1868 that a federal constitutional due process provision became applicable to the states. In that year, the Fourteenth Amendment was ratified. Part of that amendment was:

...nor shall any State deprive any person of life, liberty, or property, without due process of law....

Note that this latter provision specifically applies to the states and not to the federal government. Therefore, if a due process violation is claimed in a state case, the applicable due process provision is the Fourteenth Amendment clause, not the Fifth.

When the Fourteenth Amendment was written and ratified, it did not enumerate the specific protections that were included in the Bill of Rights. For example, it did not indicate that the *state* shall not issue warrants without probable cause. However, soon after the Fourteenth Amendment was ratified, the Supreme Court of the United States faced the difficult task of determining whether the due process clause of the Fourteenth Amendment protected those individual rights against the state in the same manner that the Bill of Rights protected them against federal action.

After half a century of cases holding that the due process clause of the Fourteenth Amendment did not incorporate those protections included in the Bill of Rights, the Supreme Court (on a piece-meal basis) determined that most of those rights enumerated in the first ten amendments would be applicable to the states. Certainly, at the present time, the search and seizure provisions of the Fourth Amendment, the self-incrimination provisions of the Fifth Amendment, and the right to counsel provisions of the Sixth Amendment are applicable to the state by way of the due process provision of the Fourteenth Amendment.[2]

§2.5   Effects of broadening the scope of the Fourteenth Amendment due process clause

With broadening of the scope of the due process clause of the Fourteenth Amendment, the powers of the United States Supreme Court and other federal courts have been extended. Where state officials once looked primarily to the state court cases for standards and guidelines, they must now look as well to the Supreme Court decisions. For example, only a few years ago the states were free to establish their own policies concerning the scope of search following a legal arrest. Now they must keep in mind the United States Supreme Court decisions. Once the United States Supreme Court has established that a provision of the Bill of Rights also limits state action, the Court then establishes the minimum standards to be applied by state agents in enforcing state laws.

Therefore, in establishing criminal procedures, including investigative procedures, the federal decisions must be studied to determine minimum protections given to persons accused of crime. Standards relating to detention, arrest, search, seizure, questioning and confrontations for identification are discussed in the chapters that follow.

§2.6   Protection of rights via state constitutions and laws

The Federal Supreme Court establishes only minimum standards. The states may, through legislation or court decision, require more strict standards. The states may not, however, either by legislation or constitutional amendment establish standards which do not meet those minimum standards established by federal courts or federal legislation.[3]

For many years, the state courts which required stricter standards than those established by the United States Supreme Court did so by way of the federal constitutional provisions as well as the state constitutional provisions

---

[2] *Mapp v. Ohio*, 12 L.Ed.2d 653, 367 U.S. 643, 6 L.Ed.2d 1081, 81 S.Ct. 1684 (1961); *Malloy v. Hogan*, 378 U.S.1, 12 L.Ed.2d 653, 84 S.Ct. 1489 (1964); *Gideon v. Wainwright*, 372 U.S. 335, 9 L.Ed.2d 799, 83 S.Ct. 792 (1963).

[3] *People v. Pennington*, 383 Mich. 611, 178 N.W.2d 471 (1970).

and statutes. However, in 1975 the Supreme Court mandated that the states, in requiring stricter standards than the Federal Supreme Court, must do so by way of their own state constitutional provisions and not by way of the Federal constitutional provisions.[4]

In the *Hass* case, the Supreme Court held that a state may not impose greater restrictions than the federal courts as a matter of federal constitutional law when the Supreme Court specifically refrains from imposing them. For example, if the United States Supreme Court finds that the self-incrimination provision of the Fifth Amendment does not prohibit the use of statements without the *Miranda* warnings for impeachment purposes, the *state* cannot interpret that protection of the Federal Constitution so as to prohibit the use of such confession for impeachment purposes. The state, by way of its own self-incrimination provision, may so limit the use of the confession, but it may not refer to the Fifth Amendment self-incrimination provision in placing greater restrictions than those mandated by the Supreme Court.

Because both the federal and state courts may, by court interpretation of their respective constitutional provisions, limit authority, state officials must not only be familiar with the state statutes and court decisions, but with the federal laws and especially federal court decisions which determine police procedures.

§2.7   Summary

Criminal justice personnel are required to enforce state, federal, and local laws. On the other hand, they are bound by oath or affirmation to support the Constitution of the United States. Although the Supreme Court has attempted to balance the police power and the individual rights, if there is a conflict, the Constitutional rights as interpreted by the United States Supreme Court must take precedence.

Many of the individual rights which must be protected are enumerated in the Bill of Rights. Although these rights, such as those of the Fourth, Fifth, and Sixth Amendments, are now applicable to the states by way of the Fourteenth Amendment due process clause, the United States Supreme Court decisions must be searched to determine the standards to be applied in areas such as search and seizure, self-incrimination, and right to counsel.

In addition to standards established by the Supreme Court, the state by way of its constitutional provision may establish additional requirements. This makes it mandatory that justice personnel be familiar with both the

---

[4]   *Oregon v. Hass*, 420 U.S. 714, 43 L.Ed.2d 570, 95 S.Ct. 1215 (1975).

minimum standards required by the federal courts as well as those required by the state law or the state decisions based upon state constitutional provisions.

Chapter 3

POLICE AUTHORITY TO DETAIN

---

*The Fourth Amendment does not require a policeman who lacks the
precise level of information necessary for probable cause to arrest to
simply shrug his shoulders and allow a crime to occur or a criminal to
escape.*

Adams v. Williams, 407 U.S. 143,
32 L.Ed.2d 612, 92 S.Ct. 1921 (1972)

Section
3.1   General considerations
3.2   Legislation concerning the authority to detain
3.3   *Terry v. Ohio* stop and frisk rationale
3.4   Application to off-street situations
3.5   Application to detention of motorists
3.6   Detention of luggage
3.7   Duration of the detention
3.8   Detention to check driver's license and registration
3.9   Summary

§3.1   General considerations

In most instances, the first step in the criminal justice process is the detention or arrest of a suspect. In some cases, the officer has probable cause to make an arrest, while in others he does not have probable cause for an arrest, but the circumstances justify taking some positive action. For many years, police administrators and judges have been wrestling with the questions surrounding the right of a police officer to stop a suspect under circumstances where there are not sufficient grounds for a physical arrest. Although it always has been common practice for police officers to stop and question the suspect under such circumstances, the courts and legal writers were, until recently, sharply divided as to whether such a right actually existed and, if it did exist, as to its precise limitations.

Although most state statutes or codes clearly spell out the authority of a police officer to *arrest*, until recently there were few such provisions concerning the right to *detain* without reasonable grounds or probable cause. This left the police officer in a dilemma. Just one example may bring this troubling question into focus.

> If a police officer, walking a beat at 2:00 a.m. in a commercial area where there has been a high burglary rate, observes a person running from the back of a place of business and entering a car with its motor running and the lights out, does he have the authority to stop the car and ask questions of the occupants? Is the situation changed if the occupant of the car refuses to answer any questions or claims that he is not required to answer questions? Is the officer subject to criminal or civil action if he detains the suspect in this situation?

These questions are discussed in the following sections.

§3.2   Legislation concerning the authority to detain

In an attempt to add clarity to an area fraught with confusion, a few states had, prior to 1968, adopted legislation defining and limiting the right to stop and question.[1] Two examples of such legislation are here discussed.

---

[1]   *Terry v. Ohio*, 392 U.S. 1, 20 L.Ed.2d 889, 88 S.Ct. 1868 (1968). This case will be discussed in full in future sections.

(1) The Uniform Arrest Act

The Uniform Arrest Act adopted by the Interstate Commission on Crime contains the following provisions concerning detention:

I.   A peace officer may stop any person abroad whom he has reasonable ground to suspect is committing, has committed or is about to commit a crime, and may demand of him his name, address, business abroad and whither he is going.

II. Any person so questioned who fails to identify himself or explain his actions to the satisfaction of the officer stopping him may be detained and further questioned and investigated.

III. The total period of detention provided for by this section shall not exceed two hours. Such detention is not an arrest and shall not be recorded as an arrest in any official record. At the end of the detention period the person so detained shall be released unless arrested and charged with a crime.[2]

This provision has been adopted by Rhode Island, New Hampshire and Delaware. The constitutionality of the detention provisions of the Uniform Arrest Act has been upheld by the Supreme Courts of both Delaware and Rhode Island, but the Supreme Court of the United States has not reviewed a case in which this issue was presented. The Delaware and Rhode Island courts, in construing the statute, attempted to distinguish the procedures authorized by the act from the technical arrest. They explained that the detention is not recorded as an arrest and the person is not formally charged with a crime.

Although this provision has not been specifically upheld by the Supreme Court of the United States, the stopping which is authorized by this act was upheld in the *Terry* case discussed in the following section. However, the Supreme Court did not approve the two-hour detention period, and the constitutionality of this section of the act remains open to speculation.

---

[2]   *Kavanagh v. Stenhouse*, 93 R.I. 252, 174 A.2d 560 (1961); *DeSalvatore v. State*, 52 Del. 550, 163 A.2d 244 (1960).

(2) "Stop and Frisk" Act

In response to demands on law enforcement agencies for a greater measure of certainty in the area of permissible investigatory conduct, the New York Legislature in 1964 enacted a statute which is commonly referred to as the "Stop and Frisk Act." This act, as amended, provides as follows:[3]

I.   In addition to the authority provided by this article for making an arrest without a warrant, a police officer may stop a person in a public place located within the geographical area of such officer's employment when he reasonably suspects that such person is committing, has committed or is about to commit either (a) a felony or (b) a misdemeanor defined in the penal law, and may demand of him his name, address and an explanation of his conduct.

....

III. When upon stopping a person under circumstances prescribed in subdivisions one and two a police officer or court officer, as the case may be, reasonably suspects that he is in danger of physical injury, he may search such person for a deadly weapon or any instrument, article or substance readily capable of causing serious physical injury and of a sort not ordinarily carried in public places by law-abiding persons. If he finds such a weapon or instrument, or any other property possession of which he reasonably believes may constitute the commission of a crime, he may take it and keep it until the completion of the questioning, at which time he shall either return it, if lawfully possessed, or arrest such person.

Provisions of the Stop and Frisk Act do not permit an officer to stop and question on mere caprice or whim. The test employed under the act is "reasonable suspicion." An officer is justified in detaining one whom he "reasonably suspects" is committing, has committed, or is about to commit certain specified crimes.

---

[3]   N.Y. CRIM. PRO. L. § 140.50 (Supp 1973). Analogous to former N.Y. CODE CRIM. PRO. § 180-a (1964).

In the case of *Sibron v. New York*, the Supreme Court of the United States discussed the New York Stop and Frisk Act.[4] The Court acknowledged that the state is free to develop its own law to meet the needs of local law enforcement and may call the standards it employs by any name it may choose. But the Court went on to explain that the state may not authorize police conduct which violates Fourth Amendment rights regardless of the labels which it attaches to such conduct. Applying the reasoning of this approach, the Supreme Court refused to make any pronouncement on the facial constitutionality of the New York Stop and Frisk Act but did not find that the Stop and Frisk Act was unconstitutional on its face or as applied in this particular case.

It is clear from these cases that states may enact legislation setting out the standards to be followed by police officers when stopping persons for investigation purposes. Such statutes, of course, must not violate constitutional standards. And, with or without such a statute, the officer must be prepared to give specific and articulable facts which, taken together with rational inferences from those facts, reasonably warrant the intrusion.

To be so prepared, the officer should make contemporaneous and detailed records concerning the activities which led him reasonably to conclude the person was committing or had committed the criminal offense.

§3.3   Terry v. Ohio stop and frisk rationale

In *Terry v. Ohio* the Court squarely faced the problem relating to detention without an arrest and laid down some general rules.[5] The facts in the *Terry* case were similar to those of thousands of other cases where police officers are confronted with situations that require that they take action. Here the officer, while patrolling the streets in downtown Cleveland, observed three men "casing a job--a stick up." The activities of the suspects looking into the store window, walking a short distance, turning back, peering in the same store window, and returning to the corner, caused the officer to determine that a further inquiry was justified. He therefore approached the three men, identified himself as a police officer and asked their names. When the men mumbled something in response to his inquiry, the officer (McFadden) grabbed one suspect, spun him around, and patted down the outside of his clothing. Feeling a pistol in the pocket of one of the suspect's (Terry) overcoat, the officer reached inside the overcoat but was unable to remove the weapon. However, he ordered Terry to remove the overcoat and retrieved a

---

[4]   393 U.S. 40, 20 L.Ed.2d 917, 88 S.Ct. 1889 (1968).
[5]   392 U.S. 1, 20 L.Ed.2d 889, 88 S.Ct. 1868 (1968).

.38 caliber revolver. He then ordered all three men to face the wall with their hands raised. After a further pat-down of the clothing of one of the other men (Chilton), he discovered a second revolver in the pocket of Chilton's overcoat.

At the trial, a motion was made to suppress the guns that were taken from the clothing of the two defendants. Officer McFadden testified that he had only patted the men down to see whether they had weapons and that he did not put his hands beneath the outer garments of either Terry or Chilton until he felt the guns.

The Court acknowledged that the question before them was a difficult and troublesome one. In discussing the case, arguments were advanced as to why the police officers should not have the right to stop and frisk in such situations. In approving the detention, the majority of the members of the United States Supreme Court were of the opinion that:

A police officer may in appropriate circumstances and in an appropriate manner approach a person for purposes of investigating possible criminal behavior *even though there is no probable cause to make an arrest.*

Thus, the U.S. Supreme Court in distinguishing between an investigatory "stop" and arrest, upheld the authority of the police officer to detain a person when he observes unusual conduct which leads him reasonably to conclude in light of his experience that criminal activity may be afoot.[6]

This authority to detain as enunciated in the *Terry* case does not authorize a police officer to detain anyone on mere suspicion. The officer must be able to articulate the reasons for his belief that criminal activity was being planned or was in the process of being executed. The Court did say, however, that the officer could give weight to his experience and to the reasonable inferences which such familiarity entitles him to draw from the facts.

The scope of the *Terry* stop and frisk doctrine was examined by the United State Supreme Court in 1972. The Court in the case of *Adams v. Williams* approved the stopping and questioning of a suspect after an informant had advised the officer that the suspect was carrying narcotics and had a gun stuck under his belt.[7] A part of the officer's information was received from an informer in the *Adams* case, while in the *Terry* case the information to justify the stop was obtained by personal observation. A majority (6-3) of

---

[6]   A further discussion concerning the authority to *search* in this situation will be discussed in the following chapter.

[7]   407 U.S. 143, 32 L.Ed.2d 612, 92 S.Ct. 1921 (1972).

the Supreme Court logically determined that, "The subtleties of the hearsay rule should not thwart an appropriate police response."

Although the *Terry* case gives officers the clear right to detain if they can articulate facts upon which to base their belief that criminal activity was afoot, the right to detain is not without limits. In 1983 the United States Supreme Court elaborated on the standards to be applied in order to justify a detention without probable cause. In the case of *Kolender v. Lawson*, the police officers detained a pedestrian on the basis of a statute which justifies the detaining of a person who loiters or wanders upon the streets and who refuses to identify himself.[8] Under this statute, if the person detained refuses to identify himself, the suspect may be arrested.

The Supreme Court found that the statute was unconstitutional, violating the due process clause of the Fourteenth Amendment because it vested virtually complete discretion in the hands of the police. The Supreme Court acknowledged that the stop might be justified if the requirements of the *Terry* case were met, but indicated that, in this case, the officers were given more authority to detain than that announced in the case of *Terry v. Ohio*.

To repeat the rule relating to the detention, if a police officer observes unusual conduct which leads him reasonably to conclude in light of his experience that criminal activity may be afoot, he may detain the person even though he does not have probable cause to make a full-scale arrest.

Since the *Terry* case, many lower courts have rendered decisions interpreting the extent of the powers granted to law enforcement officers. In some instances the lower courts have determined that officers have abused the privilege, while others have recognized practical necessities and have approved stopping motorists as well as pedestrians under the *Terry* reasoning. There is a danger that officers may abuse the authority to detain suspects as provided in the *Terry* and *Adams* cases. Therefore, the police administrator should establish rules and regulations governing the practice, and all police officers should be made thoroughly aware of the limits. If this right is abused, there is a good possibility that the Supreme Court will place further restrictions on the authority to detain.

§3.4   Application to off-street situations

Although the detention in the *Terry* case involved a pedestrian on the street, there is no reason why the same rationale could not be applied where the defendant is in a building, even in his own home. The Bronx County Supreme Court in New York has logically reasoned that the stop and frisk

---

[8]   *Kolender v. Lawson*, 461 U.S. 352, 75 L.Ed.2d 903, 103 S.Ct. 1855 (1983).

rationale must also apply within private living quarters.[9] The court in this case explained that the dangers in a closed apartment are even greater than they are on the sidewalk. The court cautioned, however, that the officers must be able to point to specific facts upon which to base their belief that criminal activity was afoot.

This *Terry* detention doctrine has a very practical application when the officer who is executing a search warrant discovers that a person not described in the warrant is on the scene. The officer in such instance may make an actual arrest if he has the reasonable grounds necessary or, of course, if the person commits a misdemeanor or felony in the presence of the officer. On the other hand, there are some situations where there is not sufficient probable cause to make an arrest but there is information to lead the officer to believe that criminal activity is afoot as exemplified in *Terry*. If there is sufficient basis to believe that criminal activity is afoot, the officer, in order to protect himself, may detain the person and pat down the outer clothing for weapons.[10]

§3.5   Application to detention of motorists

While there is no doubt that a police officer may arrest the driver of an automobile if he has reasonable grounds or probable cause to believe a felony has been committed or if a misdemeanor is committed in his presence, there are many situations where it is desirable to have the right to stop an automobile for the purpose of asking questions even where there is no probable cause or reasonable grounds to make an arrest. Traditionally, the law relating to the authority to detain motorists where there is no probable cause to arrest has been in doubt. However, in the case of *United States v. Cortez* in 1981, the Supreme Court made it clear that the *Terry* reasoning would apply to automobile situations.[11]

In the *Cortez* case, officers stopped a pickup truck which they believed, in view of their experience, was carrying illegal aliens. While the officers did not have the necessary probable cause to make an arrest, they had articulable reasons for believing this truck had carried illegal aliens on the particular route that was followed. The Supreme Court in approving the investigative stop explained that the reasoning in *Terry v. Ohio* does apply in automobile situations. The court concluded with this statement:

---

9   *People v. Henry*, Bronx County Supreme Court, New York, decided 10/20/68.

10   *Ybarra v. Illinois* 444 U.S. 85, 62 L.Ed.2d 1238, 100 S.Ct. 338 (1979).

11   *United States v. Cortez*, 449 U.S. 411, 66 L.Ed.2d 621, 101 S.Ct. 590 (1981).

The essence of all that has been written is that the totality of cir-
cumstances--the whole picture--must be taken into account. Based
upon that whole picture the detaining officer must have a particu-
larized and objective basis for suspecting the particular person
stopped of criminal activity.

In order to make a *Terry* type stop, the court explained, the officer must
make an assessment of the situation based upon all the circumstances. From
this assessment, the trained officer may then draw inferences and make deductions. In making these deductions, the evidence may be weighed not only
in terms of library analyses by scholars, but as understood by those versed in
the field of law enforcement.

Having recognized that a *Terry* type stop applies in automobile situations, the Supreme Court in 1985 considered the authority of a police officer
to detain a vehicle on the authority of a "wanted flyer," issued by another department in another state.[12] In the *Hensley* case, the officer stopped a vehicle
on the basis of information he received on a wanted flyer from an adjacent
state. Following the detention, the officer seized evidence, later introduced
at the trial.   The defendant complained that the initial stop was illegal;
therefore, use of the evidence was in violation of the Exclusionary Rule.

In upholding the stop and detention, the court recognized that the law
enforcement interest at stake in these circumstances outweighs the individual's interest to be free of a stop and detention which is no more extensive
than is necessary. The court indicated that when police have reasonable suspicion, grounded in specific and articulable facts, that a person they en-
counter was involved in or was wanted in connection with a completed felony,
then the *Terry* stop may be made to investigate that suspicion.

§3.6   Detention of luggage

Having determined that police may detain pedestrians under the *Terry*
doctrine and may detain motorists using the same rationale, the Court had
little difficulty in applying these principles to the detention of luggage. In the
case of *United States v. Place*, the Supreme Court approved the detention of
luggage when an an officer's observations lead him reasonably to believe that

---

[12]   *United States v. Hensley*, 469 U.S. 221, 83 L.Ed.2d 604, 105 S.Ct. 675
(1985).

the luggage contains contraband.[13] The Court indicated that the principles of *Terry* permit the officer to detain the luggage temporarily to investigate the circumstances that aroused the officer's suspicion. As will be indicated in the next section, the detention must be reasonable both as to time and manner.

It is interesting to note that in the *Place* case mentioned, the court also reasoned that subjecting luggage to a "sniff test" by a well-trained narcotic detection dog does not constitute a search within the meaning of the Fourth Amendment.

DETENTION, ARREST & CONVICTION

DEGREE OF "PROOF"

DEGREE OF Evidence

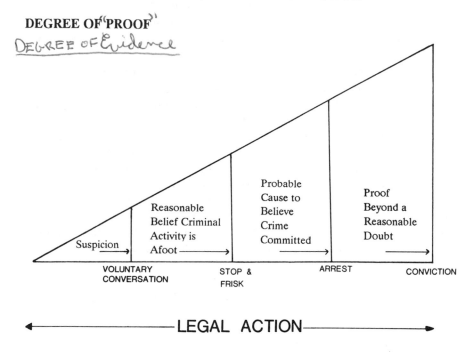

LEGAL ACTION

---

[13]   *United States v. Place*, 406 U.S. 696, 77 L.Ed.2d 110, 103 S.Ct. 2637 (1983).

§3.7   Duration of the detention

How long is too long? Although the Supreme Court has not established any hard and fast time limit for a permissible stop, some guidelines can be gleaned from the cases. In the case of *United States v. Place*, discussed previously, the court warned that, although luggage may be detained, it can only be detained for a reasonable period of time. In that case, the detention for 90 minutes was too long.

In a case decided in 1985, the United States Supreme Court was asked to determine if a 20-minute detention is too long.[14] In the *Sharpe* case, DEA agents, with the assistance of a state officer, detained vehicles for a period of about 15 or 20 minutes. They had stopped a truck camper and an automobile based on a reasonable suspicion that the camper was loaded with marijuana. The majority of the United State Supreme Court noted that, in evaluating the reasonableness of an investigative stop, the court examines "whether the officer's action was justified at its inception and whether it was reasonably related in scope to the circumstances which justified the interferences in the first place." As to the length of stop or detention, the spokesman indicated that the court must consider the purposes to be served by a stop as well as the time reasonably needed to effectuate those purposes. The court agreed with the trial court that the detention for 20 minutes was not too long under the circumstances. The majority explained that, in this case, the DEA agent had diligently pursued his investigation and clearly no delay unnecessary to the investigation was involved.

In determining the period of detention, it should be noted that the courts will consider whether the officer making the stop diligently pursued the investigation and whether it was related in scope to the circumstances which justified the interference in the first place. While 20 minutes was not too long in this case, it may have been too long had the circumstances been different. On the other hand, had the circumstances justified a more time-consuming investigation, for example, to check whether the car was a stolen vehicle, then the 20 minutes would not necessarily have been too long.

§3.8   Detention to check driver's license and registration

Until 1979 it was common practice to stop vehicles to check a driver's license, even if there was no articulable reason to believe that the person driv-

---

[14]   *United States v. Sharpe*, 470 U.S. 675, 84 L.Ed.2d 605, 105 S.Ct. 1568 (1985).

ing did not have a license. In 1979 the Supreme Court, in the case of *Delaware v. Prouse*, addressed the issue of routine police stops for the purpose of checking drivers' licenses or registration certificates.[15]

In the *Prouse* case, a patrolman in a police cruiser had stopped an automobile occupied by the respondent and seized marijuana in plain view on the car floor. The patrolman testified that prior to stopping the vehicle he had observed neither traffic nor equipment violations and had no suspicion of any criminal activity, that he made the stop only in order to check the driver's license and the car's registration.

While the court recognized that the states have a vital interest in insuring that only those qualified to do so are permitted to operate motor vehicles, the court nevertheless noted that these important ends did not justify the intrusion on the Fourth Amendment interest which such stops entail.

Although the Supreme Court prohibited future indiscriminate stopping of automobiles to check driver's licenses and registrations, the Court did approve the stopping of vehicles if there were articulable and reasonable suspicion that the motorist was unlicensed or that the automobile was not registered. The Court also indicated that the decision did not preclude states from developing methods for spot checks that involve less intrusion or do not involve the unrestrained exercise of discretion.

This case and other cases have approved the use of roadblocks on highways to check the license and registration of every motorist that passes by.[16] A New York Court of Appeals case has ruled that vehicles stopped as part of a roving roadblock procedure in a heavy burglarized area, conducted in a uniform, nonarbitrary and nondiscriminatory manner, for the purposes of ascertaining the identities and gathering information about crimes, does not violate the constitutional proscriptions against unreasonable searches and seizures.[17]

§3.9   Summary

While the laws of arrest have been spelled out by statute and court decisions for some time, those relating to detention without probable cause are of more recent origin.

The United States Supreme Court in 1968 provided some guidelines for detaining without making an arrest. Under these guidelines, a police officer

---

[15]   *Delaware v. Prouse*, 440 U.S. 648, 59 L.Ed.2d 660, 99 S.Ct. 1391 (1979).

[16]   *United States v. Pritchard*, 645 F 2d 8 854 (10th Cir. 1981).

[17]   *People v. John*, 438 Ne(2d) 864 (1982).

may in appropriate circumstances and in an appropriate manner detain a person for investigation even without probable cause to arrest when the officer reasonably believes in light of his experience that criminal activity may be afoot. This does not grant authority to the police officer to stop a person on mere suspicion, but it does allow the officer to detain when he can articulate facts which reasonably lead him to believe in light of his experience that criminal activity has occurred, is occurring, or is about to occur.

The *Terry* principle which authorizes the detention without arrest has been applied in detaining pedestrians on the street as well as persons in buildings and apartments if the detaining officer can articulate facts that justify his belief that criminal activity is afoot. In addition, more recently, the courts have applied the *Terry* reasoning to automobile situations if the detention is not more extensive than necessary under the circumstances.

Also, the *Terry* doctrine which authorizes the detention of pedestrians without probable cause has been applied in determining if luggage can be detained. If the officer's observations lead him reasonably to believe that the luggage contains narcotics or contraband, then the principles of *Terry* permit the officer to detain the luggage temporarily to investigate the circumstances that aroused his suspicions.

While the courts have not placed any definite time limitations on the detention in determining how long a detention can continue, they will look at the purpose of the detention and if the police diligently pursue the investigation to confirm or dispel their suspicions.

A police officer does not have authority to routinely stop automobiles for the purpose of checking the driver's license or registration certificates; however, the automobile may be detained without probable cause to make an arrest if there is articulable and reasonable suspicion that the motorist is unlicensed or that the automobile is not registered. Also, the courts have approved the establishment of roadblocks or traffic checkpoints to determine if the driver has a driver's license. The rationale for the roadblock stop is that the driver can see visible signs of the officer's authority, and he is less likely to be frightened or annoyed by the intrusion.

Chapter 4

LAW OF ARREST

...It is the command of the Fourth Amendment that no warrants for either searches or arrests shall issue except upon probable cause, supported by oath or affirmation, and particularly describing the place to be searched, and the persons or things to be seized.

Henry v. United States, 361 U.S. 98,
4 L.Ed.2d 134, 80 S.Ct. 168 (1959).

Section
4.1   General considerations
4.2   Statutory authority to arrest
4.3   Definition and elements of arrest
4.4   Arrest under the authority of an arrest warrant
4.5   Arrest without a warrant
4.6   Use of force in making an arrest
4.7   The citation and summons in law enforcement
4.8   Arrest after fresh pursuit
4.9   Summary

§4.1   General considerations

Before the criminal justice process can begin, a person who is entering that process must come under the custody and control of the law. In some instances, an arrest immediately follows the detention, as for example, when the person is detained and the officer discovers additional information which will give him probable cause to make the arrest. But when the officer has probable cause to make the arrest without a warrant, is acting under a warrant, or an offense has occurred in his presence, he may make the arrest immediately.

The laws of the United States relating to arrest have been developed over many centuries and are based primarily on the common law of England. Under common law, a peace officer or private person could make an arrest if he had reasonable grounds to believe that a felony had been committed, even though a crime was not committed in his presence, and even though the person suspected turned out to be innocent. Also at common law, an arrest for an offense less than a felony could not be made without a warrant unless it involved a breach of the peace. Due to the changing conditions in the United States, most states have modified the common law by statute and deleted some of the more technical requirements of the common law of arrest. For example, most states have deleted the requirement that a misdemeanor be a breach of the peace in order for the police to make a warrantless arrest. Nonetheless, the fundamental and substantive protections developed under the common law for those suspected of having committed a crime remain unchanged today and are embodied in the philosophy of the Fourth Amendment.

Although the Fourth Amendment to the United States Constitution is often referred to as the search and seizure amendment, it also protects individuals from illegal seizures of their persons, i.e., arrest. Both the expressed terminology of the amendment and the historical context of its adoption leads to this conclusion. In a 1959 case, the Supreme Court dispelled any uncertainty which might previously have existed as to the status of illegal arrest under the Fourth Amendment in the following language:

> It is the command of the Fourth Amendment that no warrant either for searches or arrest shall issue except on probable cause.[1]

Prior to 1962, federal arrests were governed by standards embodied by the Fourth Amendment, while similar state procedures were judged by a more flexible standard embraced in the due process clause of the Fourteenth

---

[1]   *Henry v. United States*, 361 U.S. 98, 4 L.Ed.2d 134, 80 S.Ct. 168 (1959).

Amendment. However, in 1963, the Supreme Court of the United States in *Ker v. California*[2] held that arrests by state and local police officers are judged by the same constitutional standards as apply to the federal government. Hence, in order for an arrest to be valid today, the police must comply with the provisions of the Fourth Amendment as well as those of the state constitutions and statutes.

In order to understand the various aspects of the laws of arrest, the discussion in this chapter emphasizes (1) the statutory provisions which give the police officer the authority to arrest, (2) the authority to arrest with a warrant, (3) the authority to arrest without a warrant, (4) use of force in making an arrest, (5) the use of the citation and summons, and finally (6) arrests after fresh pursuit.

§4.2   Statutory authority to arrest

Each state has a statute or code authorizing peace officers to make an arrest. These statutes differ from state to state and must be closely studied to determine the authority of the officer in the particular state. Some examples of statutes authorizing the police officer to make arrests with a warrant or without a warrant are the following:

> A peace officer may make an arrest in obedience to a warrant, or without a warrant when a felony or misdemeanor is committed in his presence, or when he has reasonable grounds to believe that the person being arrested has committed a felony.[3]

> A peace officer may make arrest: (1st) In obedience to a warrant of arrest delivered to him. (2nd) Without a warrant, where a public offense is committed in his presence, or where he has reasonable grounds for believing that the person arrested has committed a felony.[4]

> A peace officer may arrest a person when: (a) he has a warrant commanding that such person be arrested; or (b) he has reasonable grounds to believe that a warrant for the person's arrest has been issued in this state, or in another jurisdiction; or (c) he has reason-

---

[2] 374 U.S. 23, 10 L.Ed.2d 726, 83 S.Ct. 1623 (1963).

[3] KY. REV. STAT. ANN. § 431.005(1) (1975).

[4] ARK. STAT. ANN. § 43-403 (1964).

able grounds to believe that the person is committing or has committed an offense.[5]

(These statutes have one element in common, i.e., a peace officer has authority to arrest under the authority of an arrest warrant.) Also, although the wording is different, all states authorize an officer to arrest for a felony when he has reasonable grounds to believe that the person whom he is about to arrest has committed a felony.

The statutes differ as to the arrest for a misdemeanor not committed in the officer's presence. In most states, (a peace officer can make a warrantless arrest for a misdemeanor only if the offense is committed in his presence) However, some states, including Illinois, have extended this authority and authorize peace officers to make misdemeanor arrests on reasonable grounds to believe that the person has committed the offense.[6]

✳ AUTHORITY TO ARREST

WITH WARRANT

___ Probable cause

___ Oath or Affirmation

___ Particular Description

___ Offense Designated

___ Officer Designated

___ State Named

___ Official's Signature

WITHOUT WARRANT

Felony   Misdemeanor

Reasonable   In Officer's
Grounds   Presence*

*Some exceptions

---

[5]   ILL. REV. STAT. ch. 38, § 107-2 (1975).
[6]   This will be further discussed in §4.5.

The state and federal statutes authorizing arrest by a peace officer must be strictly followed. A peace officer who is making an arrest outside his own state must follow the provisions of the statute of that state. One state cannot give a peace officer authority to act in another state.

§4.3   Definition and elements of arrest

a. Definition

Although the state and federal statutes and codes have provisions specifying when a peace officer may make an arrest without a warrant, few of the statutes attempt to define what amounts to an arrest. One exception is the Illinois Code of Criminal Procedure, in which arrest is defined as follows: "Arrest means the taking of a person into custody."[7] Because few statutes define arrest, it is necessary to look to court decisions, treatises, and encyclopedias for definitions. Some of the more common definitions include the following:

> The term "arrest" has a technical meaning, applicable in legal proceedings. It implies that a person is thereby restrained of his liberty by some officer or agency of the law, armed with lawful process, authorizing and requiring the arrest be made. It is intended to serve, and does serve, the end of bringing the person arrested personally within the custody and control of the law, for the purpose specified in, or contemplated by the process.[8]

> An arrest is the taking, seizing, or detaining of the person of another, (1) by touching or putting hands on him; (2) or by any act that indicates an intention to take him into custody and that subjects him to the actual control and will of the person making the arrest; or (3) by the consent of the person to be arrested.[9]

None of these definitions is entirely satisfactory. *Arrest* is a term which eludes precise definition. It is a legal conclusion used to describe the complex series of events which have in fact taken place.

---

[7] ILL. REV. STAT. ch. 38, § 102-5 (1975).

[8] *Hadley v. Tinnin*, 170 N.C. 84, 86 S.E. 1017 (1915), quoting *Lawrence v. Buxton*, 102 N.C. 131, 8 S.E. 774 (1889).

[9] 5 Am. Jur. (2d) Arrest § 1 (1962).

As indicated in the previous chapter, the quantum of evidence required to justify a detention is less than probable cause which is required to justify an arrest. In 1985 the Supreme Court was called upon to determine when an investigative detention for fingerprinting purposes becomes an arrest.[10]

In that case, the Court pointed out that at some point in the investigative process, police procedures can qualitatively and quantitatively be so intrusive with respect to the suspect's freedom of movement and privacy interest as to trigger the full protection of the Fourth Amendment.

When the line between a detention and an arrest is crossed, probable cause or a warrant is required. In defining that line, the Court said this:

> The line is crossed when the police, without probable cause or a warrant, forcibly remove a person from his home or other place in which he is entitled to be, and transports him to the police station, where he is detained, although briefly, for investigative purposes.

The Court explained that this does not imply that a brief detention in the field for purposes of fingerprinting is unreasonable even without probable cause, but when there is only reasonable suspicion not amounting to probable cause, transporting the person to the police station is impermissible under the Fourth Amendment. This becomes an arrest, and probable cause is required for the arrest to be legal.

Whether the officer's actions amount to an arrest can become very important. Frequently the success or failure of the state in prosecution of a case will depend in its entirety upon the legality of the officer's arrest. For example, if an arrest is illegal, the search incidental to that arrest is not authorized and any evidence secured thereby will not be admissible in court.

Although it is difficult, if not impossible, to frame a comprehensive definition of arrest, by considering the following common elements, it is easier to understand the court's reasoning in determining when the acts of an officer are considered an arrest.

b.   Elements of an arrest

Legal writers have attempted to delineate the various elements of an arrest. Some writers indicate that there are four elements, some three, and some five. Rather than making an unequivocal statement that there are a certain number of elements, it is preferable to consider the possible elements which may or may not be applicable in any given case.

---

[10]   *Hayes v. Florida*, 470 U.S. 811, 84 L.Ed.2d 705, 105 S.Ct. 1643 (1985).

(1) An intention on the part of the officer to take the suspect into custody

The intention of the arresting officer to take a person into custody is one of the basic elements which distinguishes an arrest from lesser forms of detention. Although the intent of the officer is an important factor in every arrest, specific or actual intent is not necessary. For example, under certain circumstances the court may infer from the officer's conduct an intent to take a person into custody, when in fact no such intention existed. Hence, in a false arrest case, the officer cannot escape liability by stating that he didn't intend to make the arrest, if the circumstances indicated that the officer did in fact take the person into custody.

(2) Real or assumed legal authority of the arresting officer

To constitute an "arrest" as the term is used in criminal law, the restraint of the liberty of the individual must be either under actual authority or assumed authority. If the officer acts under actual authority as provided by law and the other elements are present, the arrest is legal. On the other hand, if the officer acts under assumed or pretended authority, the arrest is an illegal arrest and the officer may be liable civilly or criminally. Common examples of assumed authority are where an officer acts under a void warrant or makes an arrest for a misdemeanor not committed in his presence where such is not authorized by statute of his state.

(3) The person arrested must come within the custody and control of the law

To constitute a technical arrest, the subject must come within the actual custody and control of the officer. If the person submits voluntarily to the control of the officer, this is an arrest as much as if the officer had subdued and handcuffed him. It is not necessary that there be an application of actual force, manual touching, or physical restraint visible to the eye. It is sufficient if the person arrested understands that he is in the power of the one arresting him and submits to that control. The person then may come within the custody and control of the law in two ways:

(a) by submission, or
(b) by a manual caption as evidenced by some touching of the body.[11]

---

[11] *Ky. Bankers Association v. Cassady*, 264 Ky. 378, 94 S.W.2d 622 (1936).

Mere words on the part of the officer could constitute an arrest if they are coupled with an intent on behalf of the officer to restrain and if, in fact, they cause a person to be restrained of his liberty. On the other hand, mere words would not constitute an arrest if the person to be restrained turns his back and walks away and indicates that he is not intending to submit to custody. As the majority of one court cautioned:

> One person can no more arrest another by simply telling him to consider himself under arrest and then turning on his heel and leaving that person free to go his own way, than one can commit a homicide by merely telling him to consider himself dead.[12]

This last element is often confusing. Some writers have indicated that an element of an arrest is that there must be an intention on the part of the arrestee to submit to the arrest. Obviously, this cannot be true in all situations. If it were, a person who was unconscious or intoxicated could not be placed under arrest as he could not intend to submit. As a matter of law, a person may be arrested for intoxication where there is an actual seizure and restraint even though he does not understand or intend to be arrested.

Even with the definitions and guidelines obtained from the various cases, it is often difficult to determine whether an arrest has taken place. Depending as it does on the intentions of the officer making the arrest, and the person arrested in some instances, the determination is often a question of fact to be resolved by a jury. On the other hand, if the officer carefully considers the elements of arrest as discussed in previous paragraphs, he can act with reasonable certainty and avoid making false arrests.

§4.4   Arrest under the authority of an arrest warrant

The experienced officer as well as the beginning officer should consider these legal truisms: *When in doubt, get a warrant. Or, get a warrant and let the judge go to court.*

The primary and most basic source of authority to arrest, recognized under the common law and under modern statutes, is that of a warrant. This is the only authority expressly sanctioned by the Constitution of the United States. The Constitution not only provides that unreasonable searches shall not be made, but states that:

---

[12] *Berry v. Bass*, 157 La. 81, 102 So. 76 (1924).

No warrant shall issue but upon probable cause, supported by oath or affirmation and particularly describing the person or things to be seized.

It is significant that this applied to persons as well as things and sets forth some of the requirements of an arrest warrant.

The function of an arrest warrant is to protect private citizens from the harassment of unjustified arrests, incarcerations, or criminal prosecutions. The major objection to warrantless arrests is that they bypass the safeguards provided by an objective predetermination of probable cause and substitute the less reliable procedure of an after-the-event justification.[13]

As a general rule, therefore, the officer should obtain a warrant before acting when this is at all practical. The United States Supreme Court has indicated that in doubtful or marginal cases where probable cause for an arrest is not clearly made out, action under a warrant will be sustained where one without it would fail. The members of the Court noted that:

The informed and deliberate determination of magistrates empowered to issue warrants are to be preferred over the hurried actions of officers.[14]

Aside from the fact that the Fourth Amendment provides for the issuance of a warrant and the courts have expressed preference to an arrest with a warrant, there is a practical reason why a police officer should, whenever time permits, obtain a warrant before making the arrest. In most instances, if the warrant is proper on its face and the officer does not abuse his authority in executing the warrant, he will be protected against civil liability for false arrest or false imprisonment.

It should be noted, however, that if the officer's activities indicate gross incompetence or neglect of duty in presenting supporting affidavits to justify the issuance of an arrest warrant, he is not entitled to rely on a judicial officer's judgment in issuing the warrant.[15]

In the case of *Malley v. Briggs*, the Supreme Court noted that under the rule of qualified immunity, a police officer cannot avoid civil rights liability for causing an unconstitutional arrest by presenting the judicial officer with a complaint and a supporting affidavit which failed to establish probable cause.

---

[13] *Beck v. Ohio*, 379 U.S. 89, 13 L.Ed.2d 142, 85 S.Ct. 223 (1964).

[14] *United States v. Ventresca*, 380 U.S. 102, 13 L.Ed.2d 684, 85 S.Ct 741 (1965).

[15] *Malley v. Briggs*, 475 U.S. 335, 89 L.Ed.2d 271, 106 S.Ct. 1092 (1986).

Notwithstanding the fact that the court may look behind the warrant to determine liability on the part of the officer who has furnished information for the warrant, it is preferable to obtain a warrant based on probable cause rather than to make the arrest without a warrant.

a.   Requirements of a valid arrest warrant

Recognizing preference given to an arrest with a warrant over an arrest without, it is essential that the officer be aware of the requirements that must be fulfilled if the warrant is to be considered a valid one. As has been indicated, some of the requirements are constitutional while others are statutory or have been judicially determined. If any one of the requirements is lacking, then the warrant is invalid and the arrest made under that warrant as well as the search incidental to the arrest is unauthorized. The most common requirements for a valid arrest warrant are discussed below.

(1)   The warrant must be supported by probable cause

One of the requirements included in the Constitution itself is that no warrant shall be issued to seize a person unless it is supported by probable cause. This probable cause must be found to exist by a magistrate or other judicial officer. The magistrate, in issuing the warrant, must make an independent evaluation of the evidence against the person suspected of having committed a crime. The issuance of the arrest warrant results from the magistrate's determination that the charges against a particular individual are sufficiently supported to justify placing him in custody. In order for the warrant to achieve the protective function which it was designed to achieve, the magistrate must make a neutral and impartial judgment on the basis of the evidence presented to him in the complaint.

The officer can be almost certain that the defense attorney will challenge the arrest warrant, especially if the arrest was followed by a search incidental thereto and pertinent evidence was thereby obtained. The defense attorney will claim that there was not sufficient probable cause for the arrest warrant or that information on which probable cause was based was obtained illegally. The challenges to probable cause have centered around two main questions: (1) What is probable cause? and (2) What types of evidence can be considered by the magistrate in determining if probable cause does in fact exist? These will be discussed separately.

The United States Supreme Court definition of probable cause is as follows:[16]

---

[16]   *Draper v. United States*, 358 U.S. 307, 3 L.Ed.2d 327, 79 S.Ct. 329 (1959).

Probable cause exists where the facts and circumstances within their (the arresting officers) knowledge and of which they had reasonably trustworthy information are sufficient in themselves to warrant a man of reasonable caution in the belief that an offense has been or is being committed.

The key words are "reasonably trustworthy information" and "a man of reasonable caution." These are subjective and are open to review in each case.

Although probable cause cannot be supplied by mere surmise, suspicion, or a hunch of the officer, the affiant is not required to furnish evidence sufficient to establish guilt beyond a reasonable doubt. Somewhere between mere suspicion on one end and beyond a reasonable doubt on the other is "probable cause."

One of the cases that clearly held that the probable cause for the warrant was not sufficient to justify an arrest was that of *Whiteley v. Warden*.[17] In this instance, the basis for an arrest warrant issued by the justice of the peace was a complaint which stated:

I, C.W. Ogburn, do solemnly swear that on or about the 23 day of November, A.D. 1964, in the County of Carbon and State of Wyoming, the said Harold Whiteley and Jack Daley, defendants, did then and there unlawfully break and enter a locked and sealed building....

Reversing the conviction, the Supreme Court of the United States pointed out that the complaint consisted of nothing more than the complainant's conclusion that the individuals named thereafter perpetrated the offense described in the complaint. Although the officers in this case had more information at their disposal, this was not furnished to the magistrate who issued the warrant. The court reaffirmed the reasoning that the magistrate must base his decision on the information he has available when the warrant is issued.

The second question, i.e. "What type of evidence can be considered by the magistrate in determining if probable cause does exist?", has been discussed by many courts and reviewed by the Supreme Court. As a general rule, the officer affiant supplies the evidence to the magistrate who issues an arrest warrant. The information included in the affidavit and submitted to the magistrate may be derived from the officer's personal observations, from

---

[17] 401 U.S. 560, 28 L.Ed.2d 306, 91 S.Ct. 1031 (1971).

physical evidence found at the scene of the crime, from reliable information from other officers of law enforcement agencies, or from reports of eyewitnesses. In addition, informers' tips may afford an invaluable source of information for the arrest warrant.

Until 1983 the Supreme Court had placed restrictions on the use of the information from undisclosed informants. In earlier cases, including *United States v. Ventresca* and *Spinelli v. United States*, the Supreme Court had required that information from unnamed informants could be used in determining probable cause only if two requirements were met.[18] In these cases, the Court indicated that the affiant must establish (1) that the informant is reliable, and (2) that the information from the informant is creditable.

In 1983 the Court indicated that these requirements are no longer required but that the "totality of circumstances" approach is the proper one.[19] The opinion includes this statement:

> For all these reasons, we conclude that it is wiser to abandon the two-pronged test established by our decisions in *Aguilar* and *Spinelli*. In its place we reaffirm the totality of circumstances analyses that traditionally has informed probable cause determinations. The task of the issuing magistrate is simply to make a practical, common sense decision whether, given all of the circumstances set forth in the affidavit before him, including the "veracity" and "basis of knowledge" of persons supplying hearsay information, there is a fair probability that contraband or evidence of a crime will be found in a particular place, and the duty of the reviewing court is simply to insure that the magistrate had a "substantial basis for concluding" that probable cause existed.

To avoid any problems, it is preferable to establish clearly the reliability of the informant and obtain definite statements concerning the basis of his information. Where the informant has not given valid information on a previous occasion, the officer should verify the information and make an independent investigation to obtain additional probable cause.

As a practical matter, the officer should not rely exclusively on the undisclosed informant's information in any event but should take steps to verify information and seek additional information. The more information

---

[18] *Aguilar v. Texas*, 378 U.S. 108, 12 L.Ed.2d 723, 84 S.Ct. 1509 (1964); and *Spinelli v. United States*, 393 U.S. 410, 21 L.Ed.2d 637, 89 S.Ct. 584 (1969).

[19] *Illinois v. Gates*, 462 U.S. 213, 76 L.Ed.2d 527, 103 S.Ct. 2317 (1983). See chapter on Search and Seizure for a discussion of the facts in the *Gates* case.

the officer can put into the "probable cause stew," the better will be his chances that the warrant will be declared valid.

(2) The affidavit for the warrant must be supported by oath or affirmation

A second requirement for a valid warrant as set forth in the Constitution is that the warrant must be "supported by oath or affirmation." This requirement is a prerequisite for conferring the magistrate's jurisdiction over the person of the defendant. Some person must take an oath or affirm that the facts and circumstances which are described in the affidavit are true.

There is a presumption that the affidavit was supported by oath or affirmation; however, the defense attorney or the defendant may offer proof that the oath was not administered. In such case the warrant will be invalid, and any information obtained as a result will be inadmissible.

The responsibility for placing the affiant under oath or requiring an affirmation is that of the magistrate or the judicial officer. Nevertheless, it is advisable that the police officer who is submitting the affidavit, if necessary, remind the magistrate of the requirement.

(3) The person to be seized under the warrant must be particularly described

A third requirement included in the Fourth Amendment is that the person to be seized must be *particularly* described. The usual method of designating the person to be arrested is by the insertion of his name on the warrant. If the name is not known, the warrant must include a description which is sufficient to identify the person to be arrested with reasonable certainty. This may be done by stating his occupation, his personal appearance, peculiarities, place of residence, or other means of identification.[20]

Often the question arises as to whether a "John Doe" warrant is serviceable. It is obvious that if you apply the previous formula, a "John Doe" warrant with no further information does not "particularly describe" the person to be seized. On the other hand, if the warrant drafted to authorize arrest of "John Doe" includes an adequate description which will identify the person to be arrested, such a warrant is valid. As an example, a United States Circuit Court held that a warrant directing officers to arrest "John Doe, a white male with black wavy hair and stocky build, observed using a telephone in apartment 4C, Patricia Lane, East McKeesport, Pennsylvania," provided a suffi-

---

[20] *People v. Montoya*, 255 Cal. App.2d 137, 63 Cal.Rptr. 73 (1967).

cient physical description and indication of the precise location to make the "John Doe" warrant valid.[21]

The preferable procedure is to determine the name and/or alias of the person to be arrested. If this is not possible, and a John Doe arrest warrant is issued, every effort should be made to include identifying information, especially that which is peculiar to the individual to be arrested.

(4) The warrant must state the nature of the offense

In addition to the constitutional requirements previously discussed, the courts or legislative bodies have added additional requirements. One of these is that the warrant must state the nature of the offense. The warrant does not have to contain the same detail as would appear in an indictment or information, but it must include a sufficiently clear description of the offense as to advise the person to be arrested of the charge against him.

(5) The warrant must designate the officer or class of officers who are directed to comply with the order of the court

To be valid and executable, the warrant must be directed to a specific officer or to a class of officers. It might be addressed, for example, to all of the peace officers of the Commonwealth of Kentucky. It is preferable to designate a class of officers rather than a specific officer so that all officers within that class will have authority to execute the warrant.

The arrest warrant may also be addressed to a specific private person. In such case the person named must execute the warrant.

(6) The warrant must be issued in the name of the United States or of the particular state

The police power rests with the states. Certain powers are delegated to local officials by the state constitution or by statute. As the authority is primarily in the state, the name of the state must appear on the warrant, even if issued by a county or city official. A warrant issued by a federal officer must have "United States" on the warrant.

---

[21] *United States v. Ferrone*, 438 F.2d 381 (3d Cir. 1971).

(7) The warrant must be issued and signed by a neutral and detached judicial officer

To fulfill the purpose of the warrant, it must be issued by someone who does not have an interest in the outcome of the case. The United States Supreme Court has determined that an attorney general is not such a neutral and detached person, and a warrant issued by an attorney general, even though he is authorized by statute to do so, is not a valid warrant.[22]

b. Execution of the warrant

Even though the warrant has been properly issued on a showing of probable cause, and sufficiently describes the person to be arrested, the arrest will not be valid unless the warrant is properly executed. The most important requirements relating to the execution of the warrant are stated here.

(1) The executing officer must be specifically named or come within the class designated on the warrant

Today, the common practice is to issue an arrest warrant to "all peace officers in the state." This practice has been approved by the courts and avoids many problems, as the warrant can be executed by anyone within that class. If, however, as was the earlier practice and still the practice in some areas, a warrant is issued to a sheriff, he, being the highest peace officer within the jurisdiction, may deputize others to execute it, or his regular deputies may execute the warrant on the grounds that they are acting through the sheriff.[23]

If an arrest warrant is addressed to a private individual, that person must execute the warrant himself and may not appoint someone to execute the warrant for him.

(2) The warrant must be executed within the jurisdictional limits

The validity of an arrest under a warrant depends upon the territorial jurisdiction of the *issuing* official. Most modern statutes contain provisions authorizing execution of a warrant in any county of the state, even though it was issued by a magistrate in another county. In the absence of a statute

---

[22] *Coolidge v. New Hampshire*, 403 U.S. 443, 29 L.Ed.2d 564, 91 S.Ct. 2022 (1971).

[23] Ex parte Rhodes, 48 La. 1363, 20 So. 894 (1869).

conferring statewide authority on the issuing magistrates, a warrant may not be executed outside the county of its origin.

As state legislatures only have the power to grant authority to officials operating in that state, a warrant issued for the arrest in one state may not be executed in another state unless the second state has by statute conferred validity to out-of-state warrants. A warrant issued in one state may, however, serve *indirectly* as a basis for an arrest in the second state, even in the absence of special legislation. In such a case, it is not the warrant but the reasonable inference which a police officer in the second state may draw from the fact of its issuance that forms a basis for the arrest. In addition, an out-of-state warrant may serve as a basis for issuing a fugitive warrant in another state.

(3) The arresting officer should make known his purpose

Some states have statutes requiring the officer to inform the person who is to be arrested of the cause of the arrest and the fact that a warrant has been issued. When it is possible and is not dangerous to the officer, he should make it clear that he is making the arrest under the authority of the warrant and advise the person of the charge. This is particularly important if the officer is not in uniform, as failure to do so could be dangerous to the officer, not only physically but in future legal actions. There are logical exceptions to this rule. If the person to be arrested flees or forcibly resists before the officer has an opportunity to advise him, or if the giving of such information would imperil the arrest, the notice is not required. If the arrestee flees to another part of the house to hide, he cannot complain that the officer did not inform him of the intended arrest.[24]

(4) The officer generally must show the warrant or advise the arrestee that the warrant has been issued

At common law the arresting officer was required to show the warrant to the person arrested unless it was dangerous for him to do so. Because of the need for quick action in our highly mobile society, however, there has been a trend to relax the requirements of the common law regarding the display of the warrant.

The federal rules and most state codes contain provisions to the effect that the officer need not have the warrant in his possession at the time of the

---

[24] *Kirvelaitis v. Warden*, 513 F.2d 213 (6th Cir. 1975). Also see *United States v. Guyon*, 717 F.2d. 1536 (1983).

arrest, but after the arrest, if the person so requests, the warrant shall be shown to him as soon as is practicable.[25]

(5) Absent "exigent circumstances" or "consent," the arrest warrant may not be executed in the home of a third party

While it is clear that an arrest warrant may be executed in the home of the person whose name appears on the warrant and may be executed in a public place, it may not be executed in the home of a third party unless there are exigent circumstances, the third party consents, or there is a search warrant for the house of the third party. This rule is clearly established in the case of *Steagald v. United States*.[26]

In the *Steagald* case, the officers had an arrest warrant for a person named Ricky Lyons. When they had received information that Lyons could be reached at the home of another person, Gary Steagall, the officers entered the home of Steagall without a search warrant for Steagall's home. Lyons was not found during the search of the house, but the agents seized cocaine and charged Steagall with possession. Prior to the trial, Steagall moved to suppress the evidence on the grounds that it was illegally obtained. The Supreme Court of the United States determined that entry into the house of Steagall, even with an arrest warrant for Lyon, was illegal.

The rule resulting from this and other cases is that, absent exigent circumstances or consent by the owner, an arrest warrant issued for the arrest of one person does not justify the entry into or search of the house of a third party without first obtaining a search warrant for the third party home.

Notwithstanding the many requirements for the issuance and execution of the arrest warrant, it is still the safest procedure and should be used when at all possible.

§4.5   Arrest without a warrant

It was early recognized in the common law that under certain circumstances it was impracticable, if not impossible, to obtain the warrant for an arrest. The common law attempted to strike a balance between the interests of the community in protecting itself and the rights of the citizens to be free

---

[25] As an example see KY. RULES CRIM. PRO. 2.10(1) (1982) FRCRIMP 4(d)(3) 1982.

[26] *Steagald v. United States*, 451 U.S. 204, 68 L.Ed.2d 38, 101 S.Ct. 1642 (1981). See Chapter of Search and Seizure for some guidelines in determining what is meant by exigent circumstances.

from unjustified arrest. The exceptions to the rule requiring a warrant were based on the strictest necessity.

In 1975 the United States Supreme Court re-emphasized and restated the reasoning for authorizing an arrest without a warrant. The Court explained:

> Maximum protection of individual rights could be assured by requiring a magistrate's review of the factual justification prior to any arrest, but such a requirement would constitute an intolerable handicap for legitimate law enforcement. Thus, while the court has expressed a preference for the use of arrest supported by probable cause solely because the officer failed to secure a warrant.[27]

In seeking to strike this balance between the interests of the community and the rights of the citizens, the legislatures and courts have distinguished between an arrest for a felony and an arrest for a misdemeanor. Because a felony constitutes a more serious threat to public safety, it was felt by most legislators that greater latitude in making warrantless arrests in felony cases was justified. Although some states have abolished this distinction, either in part or in whole, most states still distinguish between them, and therefore it is necessary to discuss the felony and misdemeanor arrest powers separately.

a. Arrest without a warrant in felony cases

(1) Definition of a felony

Where there is a distinction between the authority to arrest for a felony and for a misdemeanor, one must find a definition of a felony. Generally a felony is defined as any crime which is or may be punished by death or imprisonment in the state prison. As the laws in most states do not provide for imprisonment in a state institution unless the term is at least one year, in most instances an offense is a felony if the penalty attached is at least one year and the incarceration is in a state institution rather than a local jail. An offense may be designated a felony by statute, however, even though it does not carry a year's incarceration. To summarize, an offense is considered a felony when: 1) the statute designates it as a felony, or 2) there is no such designation, but the offense is punishable by imprisonment in a state prison.

Some states have designated by statute the specific crimes that are felonies and those that are misdemeanors. In some instances, however, it is

---

[27] *Gerstein v. Pugh*, 420 U.S. 103, 43 L.Ed.2d 54, 95 S.Ct. 854 (1975).

necessary to search the statutes to determine the punishment before a particular offense can be listed as a felony or misdemeanor.

(2) Grounds for warrantless felony arrests

The states are uniform in authorizing a peace officer to arrest without a warrant when he has reasonable grounds to believe that a felony has been committed and that the person to be arrested has committed it. A few states add a third requirement which limits the warrantless felony arrest to situations where it is impractical to obtain a warrant before making the arrest.[28]

The two important requirements which must be fully understood are (1) that there must be reasonable grounds to believe that a felony has been committed, and (2) that there must be reasonable grounds to believe that the person arrested committed that felony. An all-inclusive definition of reasonable grounds is very difficult to come by. It lies somewhere on the evidentiary scale between "good-faith suspicion" and "proof beyond a reasonable doubt." To make an arrest in a felony situation, the officer must have at least as much evidence as he would have had if he had sought an arrest warrant.

There is often confusion concerning the use of the terms "reasonable grounds to believe" and "probable cause." Although the terms are used interchangeably, there is a technical difference. "Probable cause" is the term used in the Fourth Amendment when discussing the search and arrest warrants; "reasonable grounds" is not used in the Fourth Amendment and is a term applied when referring to the knowledge an officer must possess prior to making an arrest without a warrant. Many decisions, however, in referring to the amount of information the officer must have to make a warrantless arrest, revolve around this quantum of evidence in terms of probable cause rather than reasonable grounds.

In determining reasonable grounds, the Constitution does not demand infallibility. At the same time, the Constitution and court interpretations seek to safeguard citizens from unfounded charges of crime and unjustified arrest. However, the standards are intended to be sufficiently flexible to permit efficient law enforcement.

There are two important principles to remember at this point. One is that an arrest cannot be justified by what a subsequent search or investigation produces but must stand or fall solely on the basis of the facts possessed by the officer at the precise moment of the arrest. Secondly, the fact that the person arrested has not actually committed a felony makes no difference as long as the appearances are such as to lead a police officer reasonably to

---

[28] As an example, see TEXAS CODE CRIM. PRO. ANN. art. 14.04 (1966).

conclude that a felony has been committed, and that the person he is about to arrest is responsible for the felony.

While serving as a member of the District of Columbia Circuit Court, Justice Warren Burger, in explaining the necessary degree of proof, declared:

> Probable cause exists where the officer in the particular circumstances, conditioned by his observations and information, and guided by the whole of his police experience, reasonably could have believed that a crime has been committed by the person to be arrested.[29]

In this decision, Justice Burger, who later became Chief Justice of the United States Supreme Court, made it clear that the officer may call on his own experiences in determining if reasonable grounds exist.

(3)   Guidelines in determining reasonable grounds

The best guidelines for police action are found not in the legal definitions given by the courts but in the factual situations where probable cause and reasonable grounds have been found to exist. A police officer making a felony arrest may rely on information from a wide variety of sources. In fact, the more sources the officer can use in acquiring the necessary reasonable grounds, the more likely the court will approve the warrantless arrest. Some of the sources from which information can be obtained on which to base reasonable grounds are discussed in detail in the following paragraphs.

(a)   Personal observations

Perhaps the officer obtains more information on which to base his belief that reasonable grounds exist through his own personal observation than from any other source. The trained and experienced officer who observes suspicious acts, may, after further inquiry, produce sufficient additional information to justify an arrest. Where the totality of the circumstances, which could include the time of the day or night, the area, attempted flight by the suspect, the known record of the suspect, and other factors known to the officer, collectively lead the officer, in light of his experience, to believe a felony has been committed, the arrest is justified.[30]

---

[29] *Davis v. United States*, 490 F.2d 458 (D.C. Cir. 1969).
[30] *Green v. United States*, 259 F.2d 180 (D.C. Cir. 1958).

(b) Informers' tips

Tips from informers frequently afford a valuable source of pre-arrest information, especially in the vice areas where a premium is put on secrecy. However, the officer must be aware that he cannot *always* rely upon unconfirmed informers' tips. It is preferable to make an independent investigation to substantiate the report before making an arrest when this is feasible.

Although it is preferable to obtain information from an informer who has given correct information in the past and to corroborate this information, there are times when the arresting officer must rely solely on the informer's tip.[31] If the officer makes use of information from an undisclosed informant in making the warrantless felony arrest, he must be prepared to articulate in court that the information he received from the informant justified his conclusion that reasonable grounds for the arrest existed. The officer, of course, is not justified in creating a phantom informant in order to make an arrest, even if he is sure in his own mind that the person he has arrested has committed the offense. This procedure will not only invalidate the arrest but will cause the officer to be subject to criminal and civil liability.[32] But even if the informant makes untrue statements to the police officer, the arrest will not be invalidated absent any showing of fraud or deceit on the part of the law enforcement officials involved.[33]

(c) Information from other officers or agencies

The Constitution does not require that the arresting officer personally, independent of his police colleagues, have knowledge of all the facts necessary to constitute probable cause. The arresting officer may make use of information furnished to him by members of his own department or of other agencies. In such circumstances, however, he must evaluate this on the basis of the collective information and the source of the information.

It is axiomatic that the officer receiving information by a police radio or telephone has no more arrest authority than that of the officer who made the information available. A contrary rule would permit the police to do indirectly what the Constitution forbids them from doing directly, merely by publishing a report on the police radio.

This rule was clearly explained in the case of *Whiteley v. Warden*,[34] where the arrest warrant which was issued without probable cause was the

---

[31] *United States v. Ganter*, 436 F.2d 364 (7th Cir. 1970).

[32] *Oglesby v. Commonwealth*, 213 Va. 247, 191 S.E.2d 216 (1972).

[33] *United States v. Garofalo*, 496 F.2d 510 (8th Cir. 1974).

[34] 401 U.S. 560, 28 L.Ed.2d 306, 91 S.Ct. 1031 (1971).

basis for a bulletin sent to an officer in another county. The officer in the receiving county, relying upon the radio message that a warrant was outstanding, made the arrest and incidental search. The state claimed that even though the warrant was invalid as not supported by probable cause, the police officer who relied upon the bulletin in making the arrest nevertheless made a legal arrest and a legal search. The Supreme Court explained that if the initial warrant is defective, an arrest made by another officer solely on the basis of a radio message stating the warrant has been issued, is also defective. If the officer receiving the message had additional information on which he could base probable cause, this would add to his chances of having a valid arrest based upon probable cause.

One very significant point in the *Whitely* case was that the arresting officer who relied upon the information received over a police radio was protected from civil and criminal liability. In explaining this, the United States Supreme Court concluded:

> We do not of course question that the Laramie Police were entitled to act on the strength of the radio bulletin. Certainly police officers called upon to aid other officers in executing arrest warrants are entitled to assume that the officers requesting aid offered the magistrate the information requisite to support a judicial assessment of probable cause.

> Where, however, the contrary turns out to be true, an otherwise illegal arrest cannot be insulated from challenge by the decision of the instigating officer to rely upon fellow officers to make the arrest.

(d) Past criminal record

The more information the officer has, the better are his chances of having the court agree that he had probable cause to make the warrantless felony arrest. He may utilize the past criminal record of a suspect in conjunction with other information in deciding whether there are adequate grounds for arrest. It should be kept in mind, however, that the past criminal record of a suspect, standing alone, can never constitute probable cause for an arrest.[35]

---

[35] *Beck v. Ohio*, 379 U.S. 89, 13 L.Ed.2d 142, 85 S.Ct. 223 (1964).

(e) Physical evidence found at the scene

Another source of evidence to furnish probable cause to the officer in making a warrantless felony arrest is that found at the scene of the crime. It is quite common for the officer to locate fingerprints, a billfold, or other physical evidence at the scene of the crime which leads him to believe that a certain person committed the act. This, of course, must be weighed like any other evidence to determine if, in fact, there is sufficient evidence to furnish reasonable cause for a felony arrest.[36]

(f) Report of the victim or eyewitness

The experienced investigator will certainly ask questions of eyewitnesses or victims of crimes. The information he obtains in this manner may also be used in determining if reasonable grounds exist to make the felony arrest. For example, he may get the license number of a car used in the holdup, the physical description of an assailant, or even the actual identity of a person observed at the scene. This information may be considered, alone or in conjunction with other evidence, in determining reasonable grounds.

The listing of the above sources of information is certainly not exhaustive. Reliable information may be obtained from many other sources and used in determining if there is probable cause for the officer to make a warrantless felony arrest. The more information obtained, from whatever sources, the better are the chances of proving that reasonable grounds for the felony arrest did exist.

b.   Arrest without a warrant in misdemeanor cases

In most states the authority to arrest without a warrant in misdemeanor cases is more strictly defined than the authority to arrest without a warrant in felony cases. Although there are some exceptions, the statutes generally provide that a peace officer may arrest without a warrant a person who has committed a misdemeanor in his presence. Some states, recognizing the necessity of making misdemeanor arrests on "reasonable grounds to believe," have amended their statutes.[37]

---

[36] *State v. Callas*, 68 Wash. (2d) 542, 413 P.2d 962 (1966).

[37] See ILL. REV. STAT. ch. 38, § 107-2 (1975). Other states which authorize misdemeanor arrests even if the offense is not committed in the officer's presence are Arizona, Hawaii, Iowa, Louisiana, New York and Wisconsin.

Others also authorize peace officers to make warrantless arrests for misdemeanors not committed in their presence under certain special conditions. For example, if "the offender will flee if not immediately apprehended," or "he will destroy or conceal evidence of commission of the offense if not apprehended immediately."[38] Nevertheless, the majority of the states still follow the rule that before a peace officer may make a warrantless arrest for a misdemeanor, the misdemeanor must have been committed in his presence. For this reason, it is necessary that the term *misdemeanor* be defined clearly and that court cases be discussed to determine what is meant by "in the officer's presence."

(1) Misdemeanor defined

Unless the offense is defined as a felony or unless it is punishable by at least one year in the penitentiary, the offense is treated usually as a misdemeanor. Many states specify which crimes are felonies so that there will be no doubt as to the procedure to be followed. However, in many instances the officer must determine on the spot whether the offense for which he is making the arrest is a felony or a misdemeanor. If there is doubt, it should be treated as a misdemeanor for purposes of arrest and search.

(2) "In the officer's presence" defined

In most states the phrase "in the officer's presence" is most pertinent when determining if a misdemeanor arrest is justified. In order for an offense to be considered to have taken place within the presence of the arresting officer, he must be made aware of its commission through one or more of his senses. He must perceive the acts which make up the offense while they take place and not merely learn of the event at a later date. An offense is deemed to have occurred in an officer's presence when any of his five senses (sight, smell, hearing, taste, or touch) afford him knowledge that an offense is being committed.

The officer need not witness the entire misdemeanor, but some part of the offense must still be in progress when he reaches the scene. If not, the offense is not in his presence. If the entire offense has been consummated before the police officer arrives on the scene and order has been restored, there can be no misdemeanor arrest unless the state statute has extended the authority to arrest.

---

[38] See statutes of Kansas, Nebraska, North Carolina, Utah, and Wyoming.

(3) Necessity of quick action

Although the rule has been criticized, the fact remains that in the majority of the states the arrest must take place immediately after pursuit. If the officer delays in making a misdemeanor arrest, even though it has been committed in his presence, he must obtain a warrant. An example should clarify this point. If an officer in carrying out his duties observes a motorist speeding within his state and bailiwick, he has the authority to arrest him at that time as the offense has occurred in his presence. On the other hand, if he does not make the arrest at that time and the speeder leaves the state, no arrest can be made if the violator returns at a later time unless the officer has obtained a warrant or the speeder is again violating the law in the officer's presence.

A repetition of previous comments is in order here; some states, by statute, have extended the right to arrest for a misdemeanor even though the misdemeanor has not been committed in the officer's presence. The officer must, therefore, carefully check the statute in his own state to determine his authority.

c. *Authority to enter the home to make a warrantless arrest*

For many years there was disagreement among the states as to the authority of a police officer to enter the home to make a felony or misdemeanor arrest without a warrant. In some states, such as New York, the statute specifically provided that the officer could enter a home to make a routine felony arrest without a warrant if he had probable cause to believe the suspect committed a felony and was in the house. In 1980, when the case of *Payton v. New York* was decided, 24 states permitted such warrantless, nonconsensual entries into a suspect's home in order to make a routine felony arrest. The remainder of the states had either prohibited such entry or had taken no position on the question.

In the *Payton* case, New York detectives, having probable cause to believe that Theodore Payton had murdered the manager of a gas station, went to Payton's apartment without an arrest warrant intending to arrest him.[39] Receiving no response to the knock on the metal door, the officers summoned emergency assistance and used crowbars to break open the door and enter the apartment. Even though there was no one in the apartment, the officers observed, in plain view, a .30 caliber shell casing which was later admitted into evidence at Payton's murder trial.

---

[39] *Payton v. New York*, 445 U.S. 573, 63 L.Ed.2d 639, 100 S.Ct. 1371 (1980).

The New York courts approved the entry into Payton's home, finding that the officers had reasonable grounds to believe that Payton had committed a felony and that he could be found in the apartment. On review, the United States Supreme Court determined that the New York statute authorizing such entry was in violation of the Fourth Amendment to the Constitution. The Court's opinion included:

> A state statute authorizing officers to enter the home of a suspect without consent to make a routine felony arrest is unconstitutional. The Fourteenth Amendment prohibits the police from making a warrantless and nonconsensual entry into a suspect's home in order to make a routine felony arrest absent exigent circumstances.

The *Payton* rule established by the Supreme Court can be stated as follows:

> Absent exigent circumstances or consent, officers may not enter the home of the suspect or a third party's home to make a routine felony arrest without a warrant.

The facts of the *Payton* case indicated that the entry was made without a warrant. The Court noted that "an arrest warrant, founded on probable cause, implicitly carries with it the limited authority to enter a dwelling in which the suspect lives when there is reason to believe that the suspect is within."

While the *Payton* case did not discuss a definition of "exigent circumstances," some light was cast on this in the case of *Welch v. Wisconsin* in 1984.[40] In this misdemeanor case, the officers, without obtaining an arrest warrant, went to the home of the suspect to arrest him for operating a motor vehicle under the influence of alcohol. The Wisconsin Supreme Court upheld the action of the officers, indicating that there were exigent circumstances, that the officers were in "hot pursuit," that there was a need to prevent physical harm to the suspect, and that the public need to prevent destruction of evidence of intoxication justified the entry.

The majority of the Supreme Court pointed out there was no immediate pursuit of the defendant from the scene, nor was there a need to protect either the public or the defendant inasmuch as he had abandoned the vehicle and was home sleeping. The justices explained that the need to protect evidence does not justify the warrantless intrusion, that there were no exigent circumstances as required in the *Payton* case. The court again cautioned that

---

[40] *Welch v. Wisconsin*, 466 U.S. 740, 80 L.E.2d 732, 104 S.Ct. 2091 (1984).

before government agents may invade the sanctity of the home, the burden is on the government to demonstrate exigent circumstances that overcome the presumption of unreasonableness that attaches to all warrantless home searches.

While the Court did not define exigent circumstances, it did shed some light as to what is considered in determining exigent circumstances. The court mentioned these examples: (1) hot pursuit of a fleeing felon, (2) possible destruction of evidence, and (3) an ongoing fire. The Court also, in citing other cases, indicated that in determining exigency one must consider the gravity of the underlying offense thought to be in progress, whether life or security is endangered, the time of the offense, the time of the arrest, and if there is any threat to public safety.

Following these guidelines, the North Carolina Court of Appeals was unwilling to find illegal a warrantless arrest in a hotel room when the officers had probable cause to arrest the defendant for participating in more than one serious offense and the defendant was about to check out of the hotel and leave the area. These factors constituted exigent circumstances to justify entry into the hotel room.[41]

To summarize the decisions relating to the entry into a home to make an arrest without a warrant, this is the current rule:

> Without an arrest warrant, an officer may not enter the home of a suspect to make an arrest even on probable cause unless there are exigent circumstances or consent is given to enter by someone in authority. Also, without an arrest warrant the officer may not legally enter the home of a third party to make an arrest of the suspect unless a search warrant for the home of the third party has been issued, he has consent of one in charge of the premises, or exigent circumstances exist.

§4.6   Use of force in making an arrest

A police officer is charged with apprehending persons who violate the law. On the other hand, the officer is subject to criminal liability and even civil liability if he uses more force than necessary. The officer who is making an arrest must decide on the spur of the moment what force can be utilized in effecting the arrest, while the courts often argue for days only to reach a

---

[41] *State v. Wallace*, 71 N.C. App. 681, 323 SE(2d) 403 (1985).

split decision. Some discussion and guidelines will assist the officer in making these difficult decisions.

The general rule is that an officer who is making a lawful arrest, or who has made an arrest, is justified in using such force as is reasonably necessary to secure and detain the offender, overcome his resistance, prevent his escape, recapture him if he escapes, and protect himself from bodily harm.[42] The officer, however, is never justified in using unnecessary force or using or resorting to dangerous means when the arrest could be effected otherwise.

Prior to 1985, state statutes were inconsistent concerning the use of deadly force in making an arrest. Some states followed the common law rule which authorized the use of deadly force to effect an arrest of a fleeing felon when all other means have failed.

Some states followed a modified common law rule which generally allowed the use of deadly force to make an arrest for a felony only if the suspect was attempting to escape by use of deadly weapons, had indicated he would endanger a human life if not apprehended, or had committed a dangerous or atrocious felony.

A third group of states followed the Model Penal Code which justified the use of deadly force to effect a felony arrest only (1) when the officer believed the force employed would not create a substantial risk of injury to innocent persons, (2) the officer believed the crime for which the arrest was made involved conduct including the threatened use of deadly force, or (3) the officer believed there was a substantial risk that the person to be arrested would cause death or serious bodily harm if his apprehension were delayed.

The Supreme Court, in a landmark decision in 1985, discussed the previous rules and handed down its own decision regarding the use of deadly force in making an arrest.[43] In the *Garner* case the state court found that the use of deadly force was justified under the Tennessee statute which followed the common law rule. The state statute provided that: "if, after notice of the intention to arrest the defendant, he either flees or forcibly resists, the officer may use all of the necessary means to effect the arrest." Both the Tennessee statute and the departmental policy allowed the use of deadly force in making a burglary arrest.

The facts of the Tennessee case indicate that a Memphis police officer shot and killed Garner after he was told to halt and after the fleeing suspect, at night, climbed over a fence in the backyard of a house he was suspected of burglarizing. The officer testified that he saw no signs of a weapon and, although not certain, was "reasonably sure" and "figured" that Garner was unarmed. There was little doubt that a burglary actually occurred, as a purse

---

[42]   6A C.J.S. Arrest, Section 49 (1975).

[43]   *Tennessee v. Garner*, 471 U.S. 1, 85 L.Ed.2d 1, 105 S.Ct. 1694 (1985).

taken from the house was found on the body of the suspect. However, there was also no indication that the officer's life or anyone else's life was in danger.

In rejecting the reasoning that the common law rule should still apply, the Supreme Court made this comment:

> The use of deadly force to prevent escape of all felony suspects, whatever the circumstances, is constitutionally unreasonable. It is not better that all felony suspects die than that they escape. When a suspect poses no immediate threat to the officer and no threat to others, the harm resulting from failing to apprehend him does not justify the use of deadly force to do so. It is no doubt unfortunate when a suspect who is in sight escapes, but the fact that the police arrive a little late or are a little slower afoot does not always justify killing the suspect. A police officer may not seize an unarmed, non-dangerous suspect by shooting him dead.

This Supreme Court decision must be followed in all states. This means that some states are required to modify their laws to conform to that decision and a responsibility exists for the administrator to make new guidelines known to the officers. The Court did not hold the Tennessee statute unconstitutional as written but unconstitutional as applied in that case. In positively stating that deadly force may still be used in some instances, the court noted that:

> Thus, if the suspect threatens the officer with a weapon, or there is probable cause to believe he has committed a crime involving the infliction or threatened infliction of serious physical harm, deadly force may be used, if necessary, to prevent escape and, if where feasible, some warning has been given.

§4.7   The citation and summons in law enforcement

The practice of issuing citations and summons as opposed to making a physical arrest was first employed without statutory sanction. Today most state statutes include provisions for the issuance of citations or summons. A citation is nothing more than a written notice to appear in court at a stated time and place to answer for an offense charged.

The issuance of a citation is not an arrest, as this is merely a statement on a piece of paper. The person may or may not be arrested at the time the citation is issued, depending upon the wording of the statute which permits the issuance of the citation. These statutes are generally of two types. Under one type, the citation is issued *instead* of making a physical arrest.[44] The issuance of the citation is not an arrest under either type of statute; it is an alternative to a physical arrest. As an example, under the Kentucky revised statute which provides that "a peace officer may issue a citation instead of making an arrest for a misdemeanor committed in his presence," the citation is issued in lieu of making a physical arrest, i.e., the officer who has the authority to make an arrest for a misdemeanor may instead issue the citation and avoid all of the difficulties connected with making a physical arrest.[45]

A Colorado statute establishes the procedure for issuance of the summons *after* arrest. It provides that "whenever a person is *arrested* for any violation of this title (traffic regulations) punishable as a misdemeanor...the arresting officer shall prepare a written notice or summons to appear in court...."[46]

As is noted in some of the statutes, the word "summons" is used rather than "citation," but in either event the purpose is to notify the person to whom it is issued to appear to answer the charge against him. The citation may be issued *instead* of making an arrest under some statutes or issued *after* the person has been arrested as an alternative to custodial control under other statutes.

As a general rule, the citation does not enlarge the officer's authority to make a warrantless arrest for a misdemeanor. An officer can issue a citation only when he has the authority to arrest in the first instance. Therefore, under the law prevailing in most states today, a police officer cannot issue a citation if the misdemeanor was not committed in his presence. As noted earlier, there are exceptions to this rule, but the officer must not make the mistake of assuming such a statute exists.

Although the citation is used primarily in traffic cases, there is no good reason why it cannot be employed for other types of offenses. Where the

---

[44] For examples of statutes providing for the issuance of a citation instead of making an arrest, see the statutes of Delaware, Illinois, Iowa, Kansas, Kentucky, Louisiana, and New York. For examples of statutes authorizing the issuance of a citation after a person has already been arrested, see the statutes of California, Colorado, Connecticut, and Indiana.

[45] Ky. Rev. Stat. Ann. § 431.015 (1981). Also see Del. Code Ann. Tit. 11, Sec. 1907 (1979). Ill. Rev. Stat. ch. 38, Sec. 107 (1980). Ind. Ann. Stat. Sec. 9-4-131 (cum supp 1982).

[46] Col. Rev. Stat. § 42-4-1505 (1983). Also see Cal. Penal Code Sec. 853.6 (supp. 1983).

facts indicate a high probability that the offender will honor the citation and appear in court, the citation is the preferable procedure to follow. However, where the violator indicates that he will not respond to the citation, or where he is intoxicated, disorderly, or dangerous to the public, a physical arrest should be made.

§4.8   Arrest after fresh pursuit

Fresh pursuit has been defined as "pursuit without unreasonable interruption" or "the immediate pursuit of a person who is endeavoring to avoid arrest." At common law, the doctrine of fresh pursuit applied only in felony cases, but, although a few states retained this common law limitation, the majority of the states recognize the right of a peace officer to pursue one who has committed any offense, including a misdemeanor, across corporate lines or county lines, anywhere *within* the state if the pursuit is immediate and continuous. No state can confer upon its officers any power which is effective in another state. Therefore, the fresh pursuit doctrine does not apply when the offender crosses a state line into another state unless the *other* state has given the authority for the officer to pursue that offender. In recent years there has been a trend among the states toward increased cooperation in the area of law enforcement and especially in fresh pursuit situations. Some states have adopted the *Uniform Fresh Pursuit Act* or similar legislation permitting law enforcement officers from other states to enter their state in fresh pursuit in order to make an arrest. With the exception of two or three states, however, this authority is limited to felony cases.

Illinois is one of the few states which permits out-of-state law enforcement officers in fresh pursuit to cross its borders in order to make an arrest for a misdemeanor. There seems to be no logical reason why other states should not authorize fresh pursuit arrests for misdemeanors as well as felonies; nevertheless, this is just not the law at the present time.

Because of the difference in the laws of the various states, the officer who might have the occasion to follow a suspect into another state on fresh pursuit must know the laws of the surrounding states. The fact that the officer's own state authorizes agents from other states to come into that state in fresh pursuit to make either a felony or a misdemeanor arrest does not mean that the other bordering states reciprocate. For example, a peace officer from a state surrounding the state of Illinois may enter that state and make an arrest as an officer in the state of Illinois for a misdemeanors. But officers from Illinois do not have the same privilege in surrounding states. As the Commonwealth of Kentucky has not adopted the Uniform Fresh Pursuit Act and has no other statutory provisions extending the out-of-state authority, an officer going into Kentucky from Illinois has no more authority than any other private citizen. In this situation, the officer entering in fresh pursuit of a speeder is merely another speeder in the other state.

§4.9   Summary

The Fourth Amendment to the United States Constitution as interpreted by the United States Supreme Court forms the basis for the constitutional standards concerning detention and arrest. State statutes define the authority of officers to arrest with or without warrants, but these statutes cannot grant authority which would conflict with those rights guaranteed by the Constitution.

One definition of an arrest is the taking, seizing, or detaining of another either by touching or putting hands on him, or by any act which indicates an intention to take him into custody and subjects the person arrested to the actual control and will of the person making the arrest. A person may come within the custody and control of the law by submission or by manual caption as evidenced by some touching of the body.

Statutes in all states provide that a peace officer may make an arrest under an arrest warrant. In order for the arrest warrant to be valid, however, it must, among other things, (1) be supported by probable cause, (2) be supported by oath or affirmation, (3) particularly describe the person who is to be arrested, (4) state the nature of the offense, (5) designate the officer or class of officers to execute the warrant, (6) be issued in the name of the state or the United States, and (7) be signed by a neutral and detached judicial officer. Even if the arrest warrant is valid on its face, the officer must execute it properly.

In addition to arrest with a warrant, the officer is entitled to arrest in certain instances without a warrant. As a general rule, the officer can arrest without a warrant in felony cases when he has reasonable grounds to believe that a felony has been committed and reasonable grounds to believe that the person to be arrested has committed it.

In misdemeanor cases, the general rule is that the officer may arrest for a misdemeanor only if it is committed in his presence. There are some exceptions to this rule, and the trend is to extend this authority to apply the rule as is applied in felony cases. Unless the authority is extended by statute, the officer must make the misdemeanor arrest at the time of the misdemeanor or immediately thereafter. Unless he does so, he must obtain a warrant.

The courts have placed strict restrictions on the authority of a police officer to enter the home of a suspect to make an arrest. The current rule is that with an arrest warrant, the officer may enter the home of the person named in the warrant and execute the warrant. He may not execute the warrant in the home of a third party absent consent of the third party, a search warrant for the third party's home or exigent circumstances. Without an arrest warrant, an officer may not enter the home of the suspect even on probable cause unless there are exigent circumstances or consent is given to enter the home. Without an arrest warrant, the officer may not enter the home of a third party to make an arrest of the suspect unless there is a search warrant for the home of the third party, he has consent of one in charge of the premises or exigent circumstances exist.

Recent Supreme Court decisions have also placed limits on the use of deadly force in making an arrest. The current rule is that an officer may not use deadly force to seize an unarmed, non-dangerous suspect. However, if the suspect threatens the officers with a weapon or there is probable cause to believe that he has committed a crime which has involved the infliction or threatened infliction of serious physical harm, then such deadly force may be used, if necessary, to prevent escape and if, where feasible, some warning has been given.

To save the time of the officer and for the convenience of the arrestee, a citation or summons may be issued in certain instances. There are several types of statutes authorizing the use of the citation or summons, but in any event the issuance of the citation is not an arrest but an alternative procedure applied in lieu of a physical arrest or as a substitute for taking the arrestee physically before a magistrate.

Of necessity, the courts have had to recognize the authority of police officers to pursue persons who have committed violations if the pursuit is without unreasonable interruption. Although this fresh pursuit may be continued outside of the officers' bailiwick and within the state, it may not continue outside the state unless such pursuit is authorized by statute of the other state.

Chapter 5

SEARCH AND SEIZURE
WITH A WARRANT

In Jones v. United States, *this Court, strongly supporting the prefer-
ences to be accorded searches under a warrant, indicated that in a
doubtful or marginal case a search under a warrant may be sustain-
able where without one it would fall....*

*The fact that exceptions to the requirement that searches and seizures
be undertaken only after obtaining a warrant are limited underscores
the preference accorded police action taken under a warrant against
searches and seizures without one.*

United States v. Ventresca,
380 U.S. 102, 13 L.Ed.2d 684,
85 S.Ct. 741 (1965)

Section
5.1   General considerations
5.2   Constitutional provisions
5.3   The exclusionary rule
5.4   Extension of the exclusionary rule to all courts: *Mapp v. Ohio*
5.5   Application and modification of the exclusionary rule

5.6   Seizure with a valid search warrant – general
5.7   Requirements of a valid search warrant
5.8   Execution of the search warrant
5.9   Search of a person on the premises where such
         person is not described in the warrant
5.10   Return of the warrant
5.11   Advantage of the search under a valid warrant
5.12   Summary

§5.1   General considerations

Probably more evidence is excluded in criminal cases because of the failure of the officer to follow the rules relating to search and seizure than for any other reason. The law relating to search and seizure is complex but not impossible to comprehend. If the officer is to carry out his responsibilities, it is an absolute necessity that he understand the law relating to the seizure of evidence.

Before the case of *Mapp v. Ohio*[1] was decided by the United States Supreme Court in 1961, the validity of the search was not too critical in some states, as evidence was admitted even though it was illegally seized. However, in 1961 the Supreme Court determined that evidence obtained by illegal searches would be inadmissible in state as well as federal courts.

This means that the officer must determine, at the time he makes the search, the grounds on which he is to *justify* that search when he is later called upon to do so in court. Most searches are approved because they are made (1) with a search warrant, (2) incidental to a lawful arrest, or (3) with consent. However, there are seven additional approaches to the seizure of evidence which must not be overlooked. If the officer is aware of all of these technical grounds on which a search and seizure may be validated, he can make the determination at the time of the search, not after it has been consummated. On the other hand, if the officer cannot base his search on one of the ten legal justifications, it is better to not make the search at all. Once the evidence has been contaminated by an illegal search, it can no longer be used as evidence in court.

For discussion purposes, the law relating to a search under a valid search warrant is comprehensively covered in this chapter. In the following chapter, all of those exceptions to the warrant search are enumerated and thoroughly discussed.

---

[1]   367 U.S. 643, 6 L.Ed.2d 1081, 81 S.Ct. 1684 (1961).

§5.2   Constitutional provisions

To carry out the pre-constitution promises, members of the first Congress initiated legislation to add a bill of rights to the Constitution. Among the provisions of the Bill of Rights was the Fourth Amendment, which protects a person's right to be free from an unwarranted search and seizure. After ratification in 1791, the Fourth Amendment became a part of the Constitution and provided that:

> The right of the people to be secure in their persons, houses, papers, and effects against unreasonable searches and seizures, shall not be violated, and no Warrants shall issue, but upon probable cause, supported by Oath or affirmation, and particularly describing the place to be searched, and the persons or things to be seized.

As in the case of the other provisions of the Bill of Rights, the Fourth Amendment would mean little without judicial interpretation. Many of the words and phrases are left without definition. It is therefore necessary to look to the courts for definitions and interpretations.

State constitutions impose similar restraints on state and local officials. The wording of these state constitutions may differ slightly from state to state or from the federal Constitution, but there is little disparity in application.

§5.3   The exclusionary rule

The adoption of the exclusionary rule by the Supreme Court in 1914 has made it essential that all law enforcement agents be aware of all of the technical rules surrounding the search and seizure amendment.[2] The exclusionary rule, simply stated, is that: "Evidence obtained by an unreasonable search and seizure will not be admissible in a court of Law." This rule of exclusion is not a provision of the Fourth Amendment; rather, it is a rule that has been framed by the courts. Because it is a court-made constitutional requirement, the courts, if they so decide, may reverse it in some cases and allow some "illegally seized" evidence to be admitted at a criminal trial.

There are arguments for and against the exclusionary rule. In England and Canada evidence is admitted even though obtained in violation of the search and seizure provisions. The reasoning is that the evidence is no doubt

---

[2] *Weeks v. United States*, 232 U.S. 383, 58 L.Ed. 652, 34 S.Ct. 341 (1914).

relevant and reliable even if the constable blundered in obtaining it. By weighing the protection of individual rights against the protection of society, the English courts would agree with one New York judge who questions, "The criminal is to go free because the constable has blundered?"[3] On the other hand, those who advocate the strict application of the exclusionary rule argue that it is the only means by which the intent of the protection provided by the Fourth Amendment can be guaranteed.

Before 1961 the United States Supreme Court refused to apply the exclusionary rule to the states. In 1949 the majority of the Court members recognized that state officers in making an illegal search did violate the Fourth Amendment, but the Court refused to force upon the states an evidence rule which would limit the powers of state courts.[4] This changed in 1961.

§5.4   Extension of the exclusionary rule to all courts: Mapp v. Ohio

In 1961 the United States Supreme Court reversed all previous cases and clearly stated that henceforth, with some exceptions, evidence obtained by procedures which violated Fourth Amendment standards would no longer be admissible in state or federal courts.[5] To bring the implications of this decision into focus, the facts of *Mapp* are briefly summarized as follows: On May 23, 1957, three Cleveland police officers arrived at Dolree Mapp's residence in the city of Cleveland, pursuant to information that a person, who was wanted for questioning in connection with a recent bombing, was hiding in Miss Mapp's home. According to the officers' information there was also a large amount of obscene paraphernalia hidden in the apartment. Miss Mapp, upon the advice of her attorney, refused to admit the officers when they attempted to enter without a search warrant. Three hours later the officers returned with reinforcements and again sought entrance. When she did not respond, one of the doors was then forcibly opened by the officers so that they could gain entry. At this point, Miss Mapp demanded to see the search warrant, and a paper, claimed by officers to be the warrant, was held up by one of the officers. Miss Mapp grabbed for the paper and placed it in her bosom. A struggle ensued in which the officers recovered the piece of paper and finally handcuffed Miss Mapp. A search was conducted of the entire apartment, including the bedroom, the living room, the kitchen, the dinette, and the basement of the building. The obscene paraphernalia was discovered

---

[3] *People v. Defore*, 242 N.Y. 13, 150 N.E. 585 (1926).
[4] *Wolf v. Colorado*, 338 U.S. 25, 93 L.Ed. 1782, 69 S.Ct. 1359 (1949).
[5] *Mapp v. Ohio* 367 U.S. 642, 6 L.Ed.2d 1081, 81 S.Ct. 1684 (1961).

as a result of this widespread search. The defendant was ultimately convicted for possession of this paraphernalia.

The state prosecutors argued that even if the search was not legal, the evidence obtained was nevertheless admissible under the rule established by the Supreme Court in *Wolf v. Colorado*.[6] They also argued that the state of Ohio did not follow the Exclusionary Rule and that the Supreme Court should not override a decision of the Ohio Supreme Court. In denying the state's argument, the United States Supreme Court specifically overruled previous decisions and held that *all* evidence obtained by searches and seizures in violation of the Constitution is, by that same authority, inadmissible in a state court.

This ruling, together with previous decisions of the Supreme Court, made it mandatory that state officers comply with the search and seizure standards as enunciated by the United States Supreme Court and in some instances federal district courts. In addition, state and local officers must comply with the decisions of state courts when the state limitations arc greater than those imposed by the federal courts.

The total result of this ruling should not be interpreted to indicate that all searches are unreasonable. However, because of the inability of state and federal courts clearly to announce rules concerning search and seizure, and because of the failure of enforcement officers, knowingly or unknowingly, to follow even those rules that are clear, thousands of cases have been disposed of without even reaching the stage where guilt or innocence is considered.

§5.5 Application and modification of the exclusionary rule

Some criminal justice personnel claim that the foundation on which the exclusionary rule was built has become quicksand. Numerous cases are cited where pertinent evidence is excluded and criminals released even where the officer acted in good faith and with a reasonable degree of training and education concerning the valid search and seizure procedure.[7] Arguments for modifying the rule have been presented to the Supreme Court. Those arguments are (1) there is no provision in the Constitution which requires that evidence be excluded; (2) society and law-abiding citizens are denied the protection of the law; (3) the laws relating to search and seizure are so complex that the officer cannot comprehend them, and (4) police officers are now

---

[6] 338 U.S. 25, 93 L.Ed. 1782, 69 S.Ct. 1359 (1949).

[7] *Bivens v. Six Unknown Named Agents of the Federal Bureau of Narcotics*, 403 U.S. 388, 29 L.Ed.2d 619, 91 S.Ct. 1999 (1971).

more informed and the harsh methods for "policing the police officer" are no longer justified.

The Supreme Court has considered the arguments made for modification and has made some modifications which make it possible to introduce evidence even though previous technical rules were violated. These are discussed in the paragraphs which follow.

a. Good faith exception

Probably the most far reaching exception to the exclusionary rule is the rule that was stated in the case of *United States v. Leon* in 1984.[8] In the *Leon* case, a confidential informant of unproven reliability informed an officer of the Burbank Police Department that named individuals were selling controlled substances from a specific residence. On the basis of this information, police initiated an extensive investigation focusing on the residence named by the informant and later two other residences. With two affidavits summarizing the police officer's observations, an application for a warrant to search the three residences and the defendant's automobiles was prepared, reviewed by the deputy district attorney, and submitted to the judge. The judge, after evaluating the evidence, issued a facially valid warrant, which, when executed by police officers, produced a large quantity of drugs.

A motion was made to suppress the evidence, the defendants claiming that the affidavit to support the warrant was insufficient to establish probable cause. The Court of Appeals refused the government's invitation to recognize a good faith exception to the Fourth Amendment Exclusionary Rule and the government petitioned to the United States for a writ of certiorari.

The United States Supreme Court reversed the judgment of the Court of Appeals and found that the officer's reliance on the search warrant was reasonable and that the application of the extreme sanction of exclusion is not appropriate. The court commented:

The Fourth Amendment Exclusionary Rule does not bar the use of evidence obtained in good faith by officers acting in reasonable reliance on a search warrant issued by a detached magistrate but ultimately found to be invalid.

Two caveats are in order here. First, this does not authorize the use of evidence obtained by officers without a warrant, as for example, incident to a lawful arrest even if the action was in good faith. Secondly, if it is apparent to

---

[8]   *United States v. Leon*, 468 U.S. 897, 82 L.Ed.2d 677, 104 S.Ct. 3415 (1984).

the officers that the warrant was improperly issued, the good faith exception
will not apply.

Contrary to some comments that the exclusionary rule has been abandoned, this case resolved only that if a *search warrant* has been issued by a
magistrate but ultimately found to be invalid for one reason or another, and
if the officer executes the warrant in good faith, the evidence will be admissible even if it turns out later that the warrant was invalid.

Extending the logic of the *Leon* reasoning, a majority of the Supreme
Court in 1987 applied the "good faith exception" where officers seized evidence from a wrecking yard without a warrant.[9] In this case, the officers
acted under a statute which authorized an inspection of a business which engaged in buying and selling motor vehicles, parts, and scrap metal. The day
after the search, a federal court ruled that such a statute was unconstitutional. The Supreme Court of the United States, in reversing the lower
court's decision prohibiting use of the evidence, determined that the evidence
should have been admitted even though the statute was later found to be unconstitutional. The court reiterated that the application of the exclusionary
rule is never a "right" of the criminal defendant and the courts are to apply
the rule only when the purpose of the rule is served. Allowing the evidence
to be introduced, the Supreme Court concluded:

> Application of the Exclusionary Rule "is neither intended nor able
> to cure the invasion of the defendant's rights which he has already
> suffered"...Rather the rule "operates as a judicially created remedy
> designed to safeguard Fourth Amendment rights generally through
> its effect, rather than as a personal constitutional right of the party
> agrieved."

Notwithstanding these decisions, the exclusionary rule is still applicable
in most instances. The exceptions quoted are the only "good faith"
exceptions, and these have limited application.

b.   Use of illegally seized evidence
for impeachment purposes

In the case of *United States v. Havens*, the Supreme Court authorized the
use of illegally seized evidence for impeachment purposes if the defendant

---

[9]   *Illinois v. Krull*, __U.S.__, 94 L.Ed.2d 364, 107 S.Ct. 1160 (1987).

takes the stand and makes statements which are contrary to evidence acquired by the illegal search.[10]

In the *Havens* case, police officers found cocaine sewn in a makeshift pocket in a T-shirt worn by a companion of the defendant. The defendant's companion implicated the defendant and the defendant's bag was searched. In the search, customs officers discovered a T-shirt from which pieces had been cut and found that these matched the pieces that were sewn to the shirt where the narcotics were found. This evidence was not introduced when the prosecution presented its case in chief, but was used on rebuttal after the defendant had stated on the stand that to his knowledge the T-shirt was not in his luggage. As the evidence illegally seized was introduced only for impeachment purposes to discredit the testimony given by the defendant on cross-examination, the majority of the Supreme Court determined that the introduction of the evidence was proper. The rationale was that arriving at the truth in a criminal case is a fundamental goal of our legal system and that when a defendant takes the stand, the government should be permitted to have an effective cross-examination in an attempt to elicit the truth.

c. The use of illegally seized evidence in grand jury proceedings

In another exception to the exclusion of evidence illegally seized, the Supreme Court refused to allow a grand jury witness to invoke the exclusionary rule, pointing out that this would unduly interfere with the effective and expeditious discharge of the grand jury's duties.[11] The majority reasoned that the judicially created remedy to safeguard the Fourth Amendment rights should not be interpreted to proscribe the use of illegally seized evidence at the grand jury.

§5.6   Seizure with a valid search warrant – general

The preferable way of conducting a legal search, and one which is universally recognized, is the search with a valid search warrant. Both the United States Constitution and the constitutions of the various states describe the circumstances under which warrants may be issued. They generally provide, (1) that a warrant shall not issue unless there is probable cause; (2) that

---

[10]   *United States v. Havens*, 446 U.S. 620, 64 L.Ed.2d 559, 100 S.Ct. 1912 (1980).

[11]   *United States v. Calandra*, 414 U.S. 338, 38 L.Ed.2d 561, 94 S.Ct. 613 (1974).

this be supported by oath or affirmation; and (3) that the place to be searched and the things to be seized must be particularly described. In addition, the courts have added other requirements.

A search warrant has been defined as an order in writing in the name of the state, signed by a judicial officer in the proper exercise of his authority, directing a peace officer to search for personal property and to bring it before the court. From this definition it is clear that the peace officer in executing the warrant is merely carrying out the instructions of a judicial officer.

In order for a search warrant to be valid, it must meet certain requirements. Also, even though the warrant has been issued correctly, the evidence can be made inadmissible by improper execution of the warrant. The requirements for valid issuance and execution are discussed in the following sections.

§5.7   Requirements of a valid search warrant

As indicated, some of the requirements of a search warrant are stated in the Constitution itself. Others have been added either by legislation or by court interpretation. To some extent they vary from state to state but the differences are very minor. In any event, those requirements enunciated by the United States Supreme Court must be followed by the judicial officers of every state. For a search warrant to be valid, the following requirements must be met.

a.   The proper official must issue the warrant

In most instances, the state statute designates the officials that may issue a search warrant. This is a function of the judicial officer, and if issued by a non-judicial officer, it is of no validity even though this is authorized by statute. The majority members of the Supreme Court in 1971 made it quite clear that neither prosecutors nor policemen can be asked to maintain the requisite neutrality when deciding as to whether a search warrant should be issued.[12]

---

[12] *Coolidge v. New Hampshire*, 403 U.S. 443, 29 L.Ed.2d 564, 91 S.Ct. 2022 (1971).

SEARCH AND SEIZURE
WITH WARRANT

Search Warrant

ISSUANCE	EXECUTION
By Proper Official	By Officer Commanded
For Authorized Objects	Within Reasonable Time
On Probable Cause	With Only Necessary Force
On Oath or Affirmation	After Notice* and Demand
For Particularly Described Place	To Seize Articles Described
To Seize Particularly Described Articles	*Some exceptions

b.   A warrant may be issued only for authorized objects

Although there is no provision in the Constitution which limits the type of evidence that can be seized under a warrant, some states still have limitations on the type of objects to be described in the warrant. Those states that limit the type of evidence that may be seized under a warrant provide that the warrant may issue for stolen or embezzled property, property used as a means of committing a crime, or for contraband goods.[13]

In 1967 The United States Supreme Court determined that there is nothing in the Constitution of the United States which forbids the seizure under a warrant of any evidence including "mere evidence."[14] Following this decision, the United States Congress amended the Federal Code so as to allow searches for any property that might constitute evidence of a criminal offense in violation of the laws of the United States.[15] Although some states still have certain limiting provisions either by statute or court decision, most states now authorize searches for any evidence of a crime. This, of course, is the most logical position; as stated by the Supreme Court, "there is no rational basis to distinguish between seizure of items of evidentiary value only and seizure of instrumentalities, fruits, or contraband." Nevertheless, state statutes should be checked to see if there is limiting language concerning the issuance of a search warrant.

c.   The warrant must be issued on "probable cause"

The Fourth Amendment to the Constitution and the state constitutions provide that no warrants shall issue but upon probable cause. This is a constitutional requirement and is binding in all state and federal courts. In discussing probable cause for the issuance of a search warrant, the United States Supreme Court made this statement:

> If the apparent facts set out in the affidavit are such that a reasonably discreet and prudent man would be led to believe that there was a commission of the offense charged, there is probable cause justifying the issuance of a warrant.[16]

There is no requirement that the affiant furnish proof beyond a reasonable doubt, but he must show more than mere suspicion.

Two important points are re-emphasized here: 1) Probable cause cannot be justified by what the subsequent search discloses; 2) The facts to determine probable cause must be provided in full to the proper issuing official.

From a legal standpoint, it makes no difference if the officer locates the described property or not. The probable cause for the warrant must be apparent at the time a judicial officer issues that warrant. If those facts are not

---

[13] *State v. Chinn*, 231 Ore. 259, 373 P.2d 392 (1962).
[14] *Warden v. Hayden*, 387 U.S. 294, 18 L.Ed.2d 782, 87 S.Ct. 1642 (1967).
[15] 18 U.S.C. § 3103a (1970).
[16] *Dumbra v. United States*, 268 U.S. 435, 69 L.Ed. 1032, 45 S.Ct. 546 (1925).

available, the warrant is invalid even though the articles authorized and described by the warrant are located. On the other hand, the warrant does not become invalid (thereby making the officer liable) even if no evidence whatsoever is located.

Concerning the second point, the facts available to the affiant (usually the police officer) must be made known to the proper magistrate so that the magistrate may then make an intelligent and independent decision. The fact that the officer or others have information which would support probable cause is of no legal value if this probable cause is not made available to the issuing official.

An issue related to probable cause concerns the use of undisclosed informants to establish probable cause for a search warrant. In a series of earlier cases, the Supreme Court indicated that information from an undisclosed informant may be used in establishing probable cause. However, in two cases decided in 1964 and 1969, the Supreme Court established standards for establishing the credibility of the informant. There the court warned that an informant's tip must be corroborated, and the issuing official must be given sufficient information to reach an independent conclusion that the information was credible and the information reliable.[17] In these cases the court established what became known as the "two-pronged test;" (1) the magistrate must be given some of the underlying circumstances from which the affiant concluded that the information was credible, or the information reliable, and (2) he must be given some of the underlying circumstances from which the informant reached the conclusion conveyed in the tip.

After much confusion in attempting to determine the scope of this requirement, the Supreme Court in 1983 was requested to modify this rule. It did so in the case of *Illinois v. Gates*.[18] In this case, the police officer had received an anonymous letter indicating that an individual and his wife were engaged in selling drugs, that the wife would be driving a car loaded with drugs on a certain day, and the suspect had over $100,000 worth of drugs in his basement. Acting on this information from an undisclosed informant, a police officer, with assistance from the Drug Enforcement Administration, verified the husband, Gates, took a flight as stated in the anonymous letter, met a woman in an automobile bearing Illinois license plates, issued to the husband, and the two of them headed north to the area where the narcotics were alleged to have been stored. Based on this information, the search warrant was issued for the residence and for the automobile. The trial court or-

---

[17] *Aguilar v. Texas*, 378 U.S. 108, 12 L.Ed.2d 723, 84 S.Ct. 1509 (1964); *Spinelli v. United States*, 393 U.S. 410, 21 L.Ed.2d 637, 89 S.Ct. 584 (1969).
[18] *Illinois v. Gates*, 462 U.S. 213, 76 L.Ed. 2d 527, 103 S.Ct. 2317 (1983).

dered that the evidence obtained as a result of this warrant be suppressed as the requirement of the two-pronged test had not been met.

The question before the Supreme Court was whether the rigid two-pronged text established in *Aguilar* and *Spinelli* was still determining. The United States Supreme Court, by a narrow 5-4 decision, decided that despite the fact the judge was not given the underlying circumstances from which the affiant concluded that the informant was credible and his information reliable, the issuing judge did have a substantial basis for concluding that probable cause to search the subject's car and home existed. The court indicated that the informant's reliability and basis of knowledge are highly relevant in determining probable cause, but that the court should consider the "totality of circumstances."

In summary, the rule relating to the use of confidential informants is this: Where a confidential informant only furnishes information to a police officer to support probable cause, and the issuing official is given sufficient information from which he can make a determination regarding probable cause, it is not error for the court to refuse to order disclosure of the identity of the confidential informant, nor is it error for the court not to require the two-pronged test. The "totality of circumstances" analysis in determining probable cause is that which is now applied.

The courts have made it clear that evidence to support probable cause must be obtained lawfully. That is, if evidence is obtained by an illegal entry into a protected area, and that evidence is used for probable cause for warrant, the general rule is that the warrant will not be enforceable. To state this more succinctly, knowledge acquired during an unlawful search cannot be offered to justify the issuance of a valid search warrant.

However, if the search warrant is based on information totally unconnected with an illegal entry, the search warrant may be executed lawfully. In 1988, in the case of *Murray v. United States*, the Supreme Court again considered the application of the "independent source" doctrine.[19] In this case, agents forced their way into a warehouse and observed in plain view numerous burlap-wrapped bales which they suspected were narcotics. Previous to this illegal entry, the agents had observed suspects driving vehicles and had lawfully seized marijuana.

Without disturbing the bales that they discovered in the warehouse, the officers applied for a warrant for a search of the warehouse, giving to the magistrate only the evidence thay had obtained independent of that located during the illegal entry. Upon issuance of the warrant, they reentered the warehouse and seized 270 bales of marijuana and other evidence of narcotics crimes.

---

[19] *Murray v. United States*, __U.S.__, __L.Ed.2d__, 108 S.Ct. 2529 (1988).

The defendants were convicted of conspiracy to possess and distribute illegal drugs, notwithstanding the fact that they argued that the warrant was tainted by the first illegal entry. On review, the Supreme Court of the United States explained the "independent source" doctrine which permits the introduction of evidence initially discovered during, or as a consequence of, an unlawful search but later obtained independently from lawful activities untainted by the initial illegality. In applying the rule to this case, the Supreme Court remanded the cases back to the Court of Appeals with instructions that it remand it to the district court for a determination of whether the warrant-authorized search of the warehouse was based on evidence obtained as a result of an independent search.

The rule from this and other cases cited is that the exclusionary rule prohibits introduction into evidence of tangible material seized under a search warrant where the evidence for probable cause for that search warrant was acquired during an unlawful search. However, the "independent source" doctrine permits the introduction of evidence initially discovered during an unlawful search but later obtained during a warrant-authorized search supported by probable cause evidence acquired independently from lawful activities untainted by the initial illegality.

d.   The warrant must be "supported by oath or affirmation"

The Constitution requires that the warrant be supported by an oath or affirmation. Although the responsibility for requiring the oath is that of the issuing official, it is often necessary that the official be reminded of this requirement. If the oath or affirmation is not administered as required by the Constitution, the evidence obtained under the warrant will not be admitted into court. Therefore, not only the police officer but the prosecutor should make certain that this provision is carried out.

There is a presumption that the warrant is supported by oath or affirmation. However, this is a rebuttable presumption and the defense may introduce evidence, including the statements from the officer himself, indicating that no oath was in fact administered.

Even though there is a presumption that the warrant is valid, the defense may introduce evidence to establish by the preponderance of the evidence that the person who made the affidavit gave false statements, knowingly or with a reckless disregard for the truth.[20] If the defense can show that the affiant, for example a police officer, made false statements or recklessly disre-

---

[20] *Franks v. Delaware*, 438 U.S. 154, 57 L.Ed.2d 667, 98 S.Ct. 2674 (1978).

garded the truth, the search warrant will be declared invalid and all evidence obtained under it inadmissible.

e. The place to be searched and the things to be seized must be "particularly described"

Another provision of the Constitution is that the place to be searched, as well as the things to be seized, must be particularly described in the warrant. The Constitution does not define the word "particular," but many cases have been decided on this issue.

It is not necessary to have a legal description such as would appear on a deed of conveyance. The Constitution only requires that the premises be defined with practical accuracy. Two phrases have been used in defining what is meant by "particularly described." One is that the description of the place to be searched must be sufficiently definite so as to distinguish clearly the premises from all others. The second guideline is that the description must be such that the officer executing the warrant can, with reasonable effort and certainty, identify the exact place to the exception of all others.

In defining the place to be searched, it is necessary to keep in mind that it must be a *particular* place. If the description can fit many places, it is not particular and, therefore, the search will be illegal. On the other hand, it is not necessary to have the house number or other formal description if the description is such that it leaves no doubt as to the place to be searched.

In a Supreme Court decision in 1987, some allowance was made for mistakes by the police in describing the place to be searched.[21] In the *Garrison* case, officers in requesting a warrant to search an apartment for controlled substances and related paraphernalia believed that there was only one apartment on the third floor of the premises. In fact, it was later determined that the third floor was divided into two apartments. Before they became aware that they were in the wrong apartment, the officers discovered contraband that provided the evidence for conviction for violating Maryland's Controlled Substance Act. The trial court denied the defendant's motion to suppress the evidence, but the Maryland Court of Appeals reversed.

The majority of the U.S. Supreme Court, agreeing that the officers made a reasonable effort to ascertain the identity of the place intended to searched, reasoned that the discovery of the later facts demonstrating that the warrant was unnecessarily broad does not retroactively invalidate the warrant. Reiterating that the warrant clause of the Fourth Amendment prohibits the issuance of a warrant except when it "particularly describes the place to be searched and things to be seized," the majority nevertheless acknowledged

---

[21] *Maryland v. Garrison*, __U.S.__, 94 L.Ed.2d 72, 107 S.Ct. 1013 (1987).

that the court must judge the constitutionality of the officer's conduct in light of the information available to them at the time they acted.

Not only must the *place* to be searched be particularly described, but the *things* to be seized must also be described with reasonable accuracy and certainty. If the description of the things to be seized is too broad or too sweeping, it is not particular within the meaning of the Fourth Amendment. For example, a description which described property sought as "books, records, pamphlets, cards, receipts, lists, memoranda, pictures, and recordings and other written instruments concerning the Communist Party" was too broad.[22]

On the other hand, where the description is specific as to certain items, adding the phrase, "together with other fruits, instrumentalities, and evidence of crime" does not make the warrant invalid if this follows the detailed specific list of items.[23]

In addition to the five requirements discussed above, some states (by statute or code) require other information on the warrant. For example, states may make it mandatory that the warrant state the time and date of issuance.

One other caution. Obviously the warrant must be signed by the proper magistrate who issues it, but it must be signed after it has been written and before it is executed. The magistrate cannot legalize the search by signing the warrant *after* it has been executed.

§5.8   Execution of the search warrant

Once the warrant has been properly issued by the issuing official, the peace officer is charged with executing the warrant and in the absence of statutory authority, cannot refuse to do so. In executing the warrant and in proceeding in the manner in which the warrant directs, the officer is carrying out the orders of the court. As a general rule, if the warrant is valid on its face, has been issued by the proper official, and is executed properly, the officer is protected from civil liability. However, if the officer's activity in obtaining the warrant indicates gross negligence or neglect of duty in presenting supporting affidavits to justify the issuance of the warrant, he is not entitled to rely on a judicial officer's judgment in issuing the warrant.[24] The police cannot avoid civil liability for causing an unconstitutional arrest or search by presenting the judicial officer with the complaint in a supporting affidavit

---

[22] *Stanford v. Texas*, 379 U.S. 476, 13 L.Ed.2d 431, 85 S.Ct. 506 (1985).

[23] *Andresen v. Maryland*, 427 U.S. 463, 49 L.Ed.2d 627, 96 S.Ct. 2737 (1976).

[24] *Malley v. Briggs*, 475 U.S. 335, 89 L.Ed.2d 271, 106 S.Ct. 1092 (1986).

which, because of his gross incompetence, fails to establish probable cause. This makes it necessary for the officer to be trained in the legal aspects of search and seizure and particularly on the requirements necessary to obtain a valid search warrant.

In executing the warrant the officer must follow these guidelines:

a. The warrant must be executed by an officer so commanded

The warrant may be directed to an officer or several officers or a class of officers. Under most statutes today, the warrant is issued to a class of officers, i.e., "any officer in the Commonwealth of Kentucky." If the warrant is issued to a class of officers, any officer within that class may legally execute it. If it is to a named officer, only that officer or those with him may execute the warrant.

b. The warrant must be executed within the time limitations

Some states by statute provide the time within which the warrant must be executed. For example, the Illinois code provides that the warrant shall be executed within 96 hours from the time of issuance. If there is no provision in the statute concerning the execution of the warrant, it must be executed in a "reasonable" time. The warrant must be executed while there is still probable cause to believe that the items to be sought are on the described premises. If there is evidence that the described property has been removed from the premises, then the search may not be used as a weapon or form of coercion upon the person or premises against whom it is directed. In some states the warrant must be executed in the daytime unless there is a provision authorizing execution after dusk. On the other hand, a federal court has held that a search initiated in the daytime under a daytime search warrant may continue into the nighttime for so long as is reasonably necessary for completion.[25]

c. Only necessary force may be used in executing the warrant

By common law and under the statutes in all states, the peace officer is justified in using necessary force to execute the warrant. Deadly force or force which may cause serious bodily injuries should not be used and is generally not authorized unless the officer is protecting himself.

---

[25] *United States v. Joseph*, 278 F.2d 504 (3d Cir. 1960).

The United States Code provides that in executing a warrant, an officer has the authority to break both outer and inner doors if, after giving notice of his authority and purpose and demanding entrance, he is refused admittance.[26] A denial of admission does not have to be specific but may be inferred from the surrounding circumstances; for example, when a person known to be inside refuses to open the door.

If no one is in charge of the premises, the officer may nevertheless carry out the instructions of the court in searching the premises described. If there is no need for prompt action, it is advisable to seek entrance from a neighbor or delay until the legal occupant of the premises can admit the officers. Although this is apparently not a legal requirement, it is preferable to breaking down doors and breaking into houses unnecessarily.

d.   Prior notice and demand should usually precede forcible entry

One of the most troublesome requirements regarding execution is that which requires that notice be given prior to forcible entry. The purpose of the "knock and announce" rule is to protect the privacy of the individual, to avoid needless destruction of property, and to shield the police from attack by surprised residents. On the other hand, the officers recognize what the courts call the anarchism of the notice rule in an era when the suspect often has the opportunity to injure the officer or to efficiently dispose of evidence.[27]

Notwithstanding the statutes requiring prior notice and demand, the courts have recognized an exception for exigent circumstances such as immediate physical danger, flight, or destruction of evidence.[28] In 1974 the Circuit Court of Appeals for the Second Circuit listed three exceptions to the requirement that the officer must knock, announce his authority and purpose, and be refused admittance before he can break in.[29] There the court made reference to a Supreme Court decision and acknowledged the three exceptions as being: (1) where the persons within already know of the officer's authority and purpose, (2) where the officers are justified in the belief that the persons within are in imminent peril of bodily harm, or (3) where those within, made aware of the presence of someone outside, are then engaged in

---

[26]   18 U.S.C. § 3109 (1970).
[27]   *Jackson v. United States*, 354 F.2d 980 (3d Cir. 1965).
[28]   *United States v. Miller*, 357 U.S. 301, 2 L.Ed.2d 1332, 78 S.Ct. 1190 (1958).
[29]   *United States v. Artieri*, 491 F.2d 440 (2d Cir. 1974).

activity which justifies the officer in the belief that an escape or the destruction of evidence is being effected.

Some states have enacted statutes which authorize the issuing official to provide for an entry by the officers without the normally required warnings. These are limited to situations where the described articles may be easily disposed of, for example, narcotics or flash paper which is used for gambling records. Even without a statute, the officer is probably justified in entering with very little notice where the article sought is such that it can be easily disposed of and there is reason to believe that disposal will take place if entry is delayed.

e.   Only the property described may be seized

It is fundamental that only that property particularly described in the warrant may be seized under the warrant. If other property is seized, it must be done so under separate legal authority. This will be discussed in future paragraphs.

In addition to the requirements indicated, other requirements may be included in the state statute or code. Therefore, the peace officer should be acquainted with all the statutory provisions in his state concerning execution of the warrant.

§5.9   Search of a person on the premises where such person is not described in the warrant

If the officer is aware that a person will be on the premises and the described property is such that it can be secreted on that person, the warrant should include a description of the person to be searched, as well as the place to be searched. But in some instances the officer does not know who will be on the premises and cannot describe them in the warrant. Yet, to fail to search the person on the premises could place the officer's personal safety in jeopardy or result in the concealment of the sought-after items. To give some statutory protection to officers in these situations, several states have enacted legislation specifically providing the person executing the warrant may reasonably detain and search a person on the premises when executing the warrant. However, the Supreme Court in 1979 placed limitations on the authority to search persons on the premises who are not described in the warrant.[30]

---

[30] *Ybarra v. Illinois*, 444 U.S. 85, 62 L.Ed.2d 238, 100 S.Ct. 338 (1979).

In the *Ybarra* case, Illinois officers, on the strength of a complaint, obtained a search warrant authorizing the search of a tavern and the person of the bartender for "evidence of the offense of possession of a controlled substance." Upon entering the tavern to execute the warrant, the officers announced their purpose to conduct a search of the customers present in the tavern. In conducting such a search of the person of one of the patrons, the officers felt what he described as a cigarette pack with an object in it. Inside the packet he found six tinfoil packets containing a brown powdery substance which turned out to be heroin. The Illinois court allowed the use of the evidence, and the defendant appealed to the United States Supreme Court.

The United States Supreme Court, with three judges dissenting, determined that the search of *Ybarra* was unconstitutional and, therefore, the seizure of narcotics should have been excluded. The reasoning of the majority was that:

> Where the standard is probable cause, a search or seizure of a person must be supported by probable cause particularized with respect to that person. This requirement cannot be undercut or avoided by simply pointing to the fact coincidentally there exists probable cause to search or seize another or to search the premises where the person may happen to be. The Fourth and Fourteenth Amendments protect the legitimate expectation of privacy.

The *Ybarra* case stands for the proposition that a warrant which describes the premises only does not justify the search of persons on the premises *under the warrant*. As will be discussed in future paragraphs, the frisk or search of the person may be justified if there are grounds to believe criminal activity is afoot or if the authority exists to make the arrest of the person. Also, at least one court has determined that a warrant authorizing the search of a house and "any person present" was properly issued to law enforcement officers who had reason to believe that a robbery suspect had hidden the proceeds of the crime inside the house prior to the arrest.[31]

Another court found it reasonable to detain a person who occupied the premises for which a search warrant was issued and to conduct a search of that person for the protection of the officer. The court concluded here that the brief detention of a resident who occupied the premises was a limited additional burden attending the search authorized by a search warrant.[32]

If proper preparations are made prior to the search and all available facts concerning the possibility of persons on the premises made available to

---

[31]   *United States v. Graham*, 563 F.Supp. 149 (D.C. NY 1983).
[32]   *Michigan v. Summer*, 452 U.S. 692, 69 L.Ed.2d 340, 101 S.Ct. 2587 (1981).

the issuing official, there is a good chance that a constitutional challenge at a later date will be avoided.

§5.10   Return of the warrant

The final step for the officer in carrying out the orders of the court is to return the warrant, with the results of its execution, to the court or to a designated agency. The return should list the items particularly described in the search warrant, and indicate when and where these items were seized. Generally, a copy of the inventory is forwarded to the person from whose premises the instruments, articles, or things were taken, and to the applicant for the warrant.

Some statutes contain provisions indicating the amount of time the officer has before the warrant must be returned. In other states, the provisions are that the return shall be made without unnecessary delay. Although there is some indication that failure to comply strictly with the statute will not make the warrant void, good procedure would indicate that the requirements should be followed.

§5.11   Advantages of the search under a valid warrant

Although the courts have recognized the necessity of authorizing searches without a warrant, the preferable method is under the authority of a judicially issued warrant. Some of these advantages are apparent.

a.   The evidence obtained under the warrant is more likely to be admitted

The courts have made it quite clear that they are encouraging the use of search warrants in preference to searches without the warrant. In the case of *United States v. Ventresca*,[33] the warrantless search was not approved, but the Court intimated that had the proper course of obtaining a warrant from a magistrate been followed and had the magistrate on the same evidence available to the police made a finding of probable cause, the search would have been sustained.

---

[33]   380 U.S. 102, 13 L.Ed.2d 684, 85 S.Ct. 741 (1965).

b. *The officer generally is protected when the search warrant is used*

As a general rule, the officer acting under a search warrant is protected from civil and criminal liability even though it turns out that the search warrant was incorrectly issued. As pointed out earlier, if the activity of the officer who presents the supporting affidavit indicates gross incompetence or neglect of duty in presenting such information, he is not entitled to rely on a judicial officer's judgment in issuing the warrant.

Also, it is apparent that if the officer who presents affidavits to justify the issuance of the warrant intentionally gives incorrect or untrue statements, he may be subject to civil liability.

§5.12   Summary

The Fourth Amendment to the United States Constitution was added in 1791 to protect persons, houses, papers and effects against unreasonable searches and seizures. This Amendment also provides that no warrant shall issue except on probable cause, supported by oath or affirmation, and particularly describing the place to be searched or the persons or things to be seized.

The Constitution contains no provision concerning the exclusion of evidence obtained in violation of the provisions of the Amendment. On the other hand, the United States Supreme Court has by court decision established the rule that evidence obtained in violation of the provisions of the Constitution, with some exceptions, will not be admissible in either federal or state court.

In recent years, the Supreme Court has recognized what has come to be known as a good faith exception to the exclusionary rule. In applying this exception, the Court has resolved that the Fourth Amendment exclusionary rule does not bar the use of evidence obtained in good faith by officers acting in reasonable reliance on a search warrant issued by a detached magistrate but ultimately found to be invalid. This exception applied only where the officer acts under a warrant. Courts have also recognized exception to the exclusionary rule where the evidence seized is used for impeachment purposes and not for the prosecution's case in chief.

The preferable means of making search is with a search warrant. For a search warrant to be valid, the court-established requirements must be met. These are: (1) a proper official must issue the warrant, (2) a warrant must be issued only for certain objects, (3) the warrant must be issued on probable cause, (4) the warrant must be supported by oath or affirmation, and (5) the place to be searched and the things to be seized must be particularly described. Some states add additional requirements.

In establishing probable cause, information from an informant may be used without disclosing the name of the informant. However, sufficient information must be given to the issuing official so that, considering the totality of circumstances, the official can make a practical, common-sense decision from the circumstances that contraband or evidence of the crime will be in a particular place.

If the search is to be legal and the evidence admissible, the officer must follow certain rules in executing the warrant. These include: (1) the warrant must be executed by the officer or officers so commanded or be within the class designated; (2) the warrant must be executed within the time limitations; (3) only necessary force may be used in executing the warrant; (4) usually prior notice and demand should proceed entry; and (5) only the property described in the warrant may be seized under the warrant.

In executing the warrant only the premises and persons described in the warrant may be searched under the warrant. However, search of persons on the premises may be justified under exceptions which are described in the following chapter.

Chapter 6

SEARCH AND SEIZURE WITHOUT A WARRANT

It is unreasonable searches that are prohibited by the Fourth Amendment. It was recognized by the framers of the Constitution that there were reasonable searches for which no warrant was required...The right to search a person incident to the arrest always has been recognized in this country and in England.

United States v. Rabinowitz,
339 U.S. 56, 94 L.Ed.2d 653,
70 S. Ct. 430 (1950)

Section
6.1   General considerations
6.2   Search incidental to a lawful arrest
6.3   Search with a valid waiver
6.4   Search of movable vehicles and objects
6.5   Seizure without a search (plain view)
6.6   Search by a private individual
6.7   Search of premises not protected by the
       Fourth Amendment (open fields)
6.8   Standing to challenge the search

SEARCH AND SEIZURE PEGS

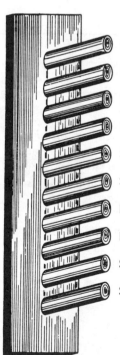

SEARCH WARRANT

INCIDENT TO LAWFUL ARREST

WAIVER OF RIGHTS

SEARCH OF MOVABLE VEHICLES OR OBJECTS

SEIZURE WITHOUT A SEARCH (PLAIN VIEW)

SEIZURE BY PRIVATE INDIVIDUAL

PREMISES NOT CONSTITUTIONALLY PROTECTED (OPEN FIELDS)

NO STANDING TO CHALLENGE

SEARCH AFTER LAWFUL IMPOUNDMENT

STOP AND FRISK SEIZURES

6.9   Search after lawful impoundment (inventory searches)
6.10   Stop and frisk seizures
6.11   Search of pervasively regulated business
6.12   Seizure of verbal evidence via concealed recorders or microphones
6.13   Summary

§6.1   General considerations

There are no provisions in the Fourth Amendment specifically authorizing a search without a warrant. However, the courts have long recognized exceptions and have, on the basis of necessity, approved searches without a warrant. Although the exception rules have been modified in recent years, the instances where searches can be made without a warrant can be defined, enumerated and explained. If a warrantless search does not come within one of the specific exceptions discussed here, the search probably will be considered illegal and evidence obtained inadmissible for most evidentiary purposes.

While the respective states may recognize and adopt those exceptions approved by the United States Supreme Court, these states may not by court action or legislation add exceptions that have not been recognized by the Supreme Court. On the other hand, the state courts or legislatures may limit the number of exceptions. For example, all state courts have recognized the search of a person incidental to a lawful arrest exception to the warrant requirement. But some state courts limit the search to a search for weapons or fruits of the crime for which the arrest was made, even though this limitation has not been required by the United States Supreme Court.[1]

§6.2   Search incidental to a lawful arrest

a.   Rationale for exception

The search incidental to a lawful arrest was one of the early recognized exceptions to the rule that a search must be made under a search warrant. In practice, more searches are carried out under this exception than by way of the warrant. It is quite obvious that the authority to search incidental to a lawful arrest is necessary, as it is impractical to obtain warrants in all instances.

---

[1]   *State v. Kaluna*, 55 Haw. 361, 520 P.2d 51 (1974).

A search incidental to a lawful arrest is permitted for two reasons: (1) to protect the arresting officer by depriving the arrestee of potential means of escape, and (2) to avoid destruction of evidence by the arrested person.

If the reasoning for the search incidental to a lawful arrest is comprehended, few problems will arise when applying this exception.

b. Requirements

Before a search can be made as an incident to a lawful arrest, certain requirements, as established by the courts, must be met. These requirements are discussed in the following paragraphs.

(1) The arrest must be lawful

The first and most important requirement is that the arrest itself be a lawful one. If the arrest is not lawful, all that follows, including the resulting search, is unlawful, and evidence so obtained is inadmissible except in those rare cases discussed in the previous chapters.

(2) Only certain articles may be seized

Some states by statute or court decision still restrict the seizure incidental to a lawful arrest to the fruits of the crime, means by which it was committed, and weapons to effect an escape. In those states, mere evidence, i.e., evidence that does not come within the three categories, cannot be seized with a warrant or incidental to an arrest. Some states have logically expanded this to include seizure of any evidence which has been used in commission of a crime or which may constitute evidence of any crime.[2]

The United States Supreme Court in a 1967 opinion made it clear that there is no constitutional demand that the seizure be limited to certain articles.[3] In that case the majority overruled previous decisions and held that there was no constitutional prohibition concerning the seizure of "mere evidence."

Although the United States Congress has modified the federal statutory provisions concerning the search of any evidence, some state legislatures have neglected to do so. Therefore, the state officer must consult the state statutes and state decisions to determine if there are any restrictions relating to articles which can be seized incidental to a lawful arrest.

---

[2]   Ill. Rev. Stat. ch. 38, § 108-1 (1980).

[3]   *Warden v. Hayden*, 387 U.S. 294, 18 L.Ed.2d 782, 87 S.Ct. 1642 (1967).

(3) The search must be made contemporaneously with the arrest

In discussing the rationale for the search incidental to a lawful arrest exception, it was pointed out that the exception is recognized for two purposes: (1) to protect the officer, and (2) to avoid destruction of evidence. If the suspect is arrested and secured, so that there is no danger to the officer and the suspect has no opportunity to destroy or hide evidence, the reason for the rule no longer exists. Therefore, the search must be made contemporaneously with the arrest. In one Kentucky case, the Court of Appeals determined that if the arresting officer has arrested the suspect, searched him, handcuffed him, and placed him in another car, there can be no search of the other car or the vicinity as an incident to an arrest.[4]

The courts have not been consistent in determining what is contemporaneous. There is no problem if there is in fact a physical arrest and the search immediately follows that arrest. But as the arrest confers the power to make the incidental search, there is some question concerning a search made just prior to the time the person is officially placed under arrest. If the circumstances are such that advising the suspect that he is "under arrest" reasonably could be dangerous to the officer or result in the destruction of evidence, some courts have held that the search may precede the formal arrest "as long as probable cause to arrest existed at the time of the search."[5] In any event, the officer cannot make the arrest and transport the suspect to the jail and then return and search the area as an incident to that arrest. In this situation, the justification for the incidental search just does not exist.[6] To avoid any problems, the best practice is to advise the person apprehended that he is being arrested, and to make the contemporaneous search immediately or as soon as practicable.

(4) The arrest must be in good faith

If the arrest is a sham or subterfuge, even though it is supported by probable cause, the incidental search will not be upheld. For example, if an officer stops a car ostensibly to arrest the person for driving with one headlight out but in fact for the purpose of searching the driver, this search will be suspect. If the court is convinced that the arrest was a hoax or a subterfuge in order to make the search, the use of evidence obtained as a result of this

---

[4]   *Lane v. Commonwealth*, 386 S.W.2d 743 (Ky. 1965).

[5]   *United States v. Jenkins*, 496 F.2d 57 (2d Cir. 1974).

[6]   *Dixon v. State*, 23 Md.App. 19, 327 A.2d 516 (1974).

search will generally be inadmissible. This is especially true if the minor charge on which the arrest was made is later dropped.[7]

c.   Area of search

Even if the arrest is lawful, the incidental search is limited in geographic scope. After more than forty years of indecision concerning the scope of the search incidental to a lawful arrest, the United States Supreme Court in 1969 finally defined the scope with reasonable accuracy.[8] In the *Chimel* case the Supreme Court held that a search incidental to a lawful arrest is limited to the arrestee's person and to the area from which he might obtain either a weapon or something that can be used as evidence against him. The facts of the case are not unusual. Police officers had arrested the petitioner with an arrest warrant and incidental to that arrest for burglary made a physical search of the entire premises. The Court specifically reaffirmed the authority of a peace officer to conduct a search incidental to a lawful arrest but limited the scope of such search. The Court, in establishing the proper extent of a search incidental to a lawful arrest, noted:

> When an arrest is made it is reasonable for the arresting officer to search the person arrested in order to remove any weapons that the latter might seek to use in order to resist arrest or effect his escape.

Again, the Court in defining the scope made this comment:

> There is ample justification, therefore, for a search of the arrestee's person and the area within his immediate control--construing that phrase to mean the area from which he might gain possession of a weapon or destructible evidence.

To summarize, the Supreme Court has determined that when a legal arrest is made, the arresting officer or officers may search the *person* of the defendant for weapons or evidence and in addition may search the area into which the defendant might *reach* to obtain a weapon or to destroy or conceal evidence.

Even with this definition of the area of scope, some questions are left unanswered. For example, what is meant by the term "reach" or "gain posses-

---

[7] *United States v. Pampinella*, 131 F.Supp.595 (N.D. Ill. 1955).
[8] *Chimel v. California*, 395 U.S. 752, 23 L.Ed.2d 685, 89 S.Ct. 2034 (1969).

sion?" Some terms that have been used by courts in discussing the area of search are "wing span" and "within the lunge area."[9]

In applying the rules established in the *Chimel* case, many factors will be considered by the reviewing courts. For example, if the arrestee is handcuffed, the reach or lunge area is more limited than if he is not handcuffed. Also, it is reasonable to consider the type of evidence to be seized and even the physical agility of the arrestee. If the reason for the rule is considered, the application will be less difficult.

To explain more fully the perimeters of search incidental to a lawful arrest, specific situations will be discussed.

(1) Search of the person arrested

In *Chimel*, the Court clearly indicated that the arresting officer may search for and seize any evidence on the arrestee's person to prevent its concealment or destruction. But does this empower the arresting officer to search thoroughly every person he arrests regardless of the charge? In the case of *United States v. Robinson*, the question presented was whether a full search could legitimately follow an arrest for a traffic violation.[10] In rejecting the argument that the search incidental to a lawful arrest depends upon the probability of discovering fruits or further evidence of the particular crime for which the arrest is made, the Supreme Court upheld the full search of the person arrested. The justice explained that the justification for the authority to search incidental to a lawful arrest rests as much on the need to disarm the suspect in order to take him into custody as it does on the need to preserve evidence on his person for later use at trial.

Although there are some state decisions which limit the scope of search under the circumstances described in *Robinson*, the majority rule which now exists is that an officer who has proper authority to make an arrest may make a full search of the arrestee, and seize evidence from the person of the arrestee even though such evidence has no direct connection with the arrest.[11]

---

[9] *Scott v. State*, 7 Md.App. 505, 256 A.2d 384 (1969).

[10] 414 U.S. 218, 38 L.Ed.2d 427, 94 S.Ct. 467 (1973). Also see *Gustafson v. Florida*, 414 U.S. 260, 38 L.Ed.2d 456, 94 S.Ct. 488 (1973).

[11] For states which do not follow the *Robinson* rule, see *State v. Kaluna*, 55 Haw. 361, 520 P.2d 51 (1974) and *State v. Florance*, 270 Ore. 169, 527 P.2d 1202 (1974).

(2) Search of arrestee's clothing

A practical question that often confronts the arresting officer is whether he can search the clothing of the arrestee after he has been lodged in jail. In a 1974 case, the United States Supreme Court again expressed the view that the Fourth Amendment prohibits only unreasonable searches and approved the search of the clothing of the person after he had been arrested and placed in jail. In upholding this examination of the clothing, the United States Supreme Court stated:

> Once an accused is lawfully arrested and in custody, the effects in his possession at the place of detention that were subject to search at the time and place of his arrest may lawfully be searched and seized without a warrant even though a substantial period of time has elapsed between the arrest and the subsequent administrative processing, on the one hand, and the taking of property for use as evidence on the other.[12]

The Court cautioned that the decision is limited to the facts of that case and that there is a time when the Fourth Amendment would prohibit post-arrest seizures of the effects of the arrestee. But in this case the Court held that the seizure of the clothes was reasonable under the circumstances.

(3) Search of premises where the arrest was made

Although cases prior to 1969 held that the search of the entire dwelling place was justified as an incident to a lawful arrest where the arrest was made in the living room, the *Chimel* ruling overturned that reasoning. But under the rule formulated in *Chimel*, the search, even inside the dwelling, is limited to the area where the arrestee might reach or lunge in order to obtain a weapon or conceal or destroy evidence. In some instances, other evidence may be seized or other parts of the house searched, but not as an incident to that lawful arrest.

The United States Supreme Court in 1978 and again in 1984 reiterated the rule that an arrest in an apartment does not justify the search of the whole apartment incident to that arrest.[13]

---

[12] *United States v. Edwards*, 415 U.S. 800, 39 L.Ed.2d 771, 94 S.Ct. 1234 (1974).

[13] *Mincey v. Arizona*, 437 U.S. 385, 57 L.Ed.2d 290, 98 S.Ct. 2408 (1978; *Thompson v. Louisiana*, 469 U.S. 17, 83 L.Ed.2d 246, 105 S.Ct. 409 (1984).

In the *Mincey* case, an undercover officer was shot and killed during a narcotics raid on the defendant's apartment. The investigating officers arrested the defendant and searched the apartment for four days during which time the entire apartment was search, photographed, and diagrammed. The officers opened drawers, closets, and cupboards and inspected their contents. They even pulled up sections of the carpet and removed them for examination. No warrant was obtained, but the evidence, including the bullets and shell casings, guns, narcotics and narcotic paraphernalia, was used at the trial where the defendant was found guilty of murder, assault, and narcotics violation.

The Supreme Court refused to justify this search as an incident to a lawful arrest and refused to add a "murder exception" to the list of searches justified without a warrant. The Court indicated there was no objection to warrantless entries when officers believe that a person within the premises is in need of immediate aid. Also, when police officers come upon the scene of a homicide they may make a prompt, warrantless search of the premises to see if there are other victims or if the killer is still on the premises. While making the search for victims or other persons involved, the police may seize evidence that is in plain view during the course of these emergency activities.

The Court insisted, however, that there was no indication in this case that evidence would be lost, destroyed, or removed during the time required to obtain a search warrant, and there was no suggestion that a search warrant could not have been obtained easily and conveniently.

In the case of *Thompson v. Louisiana* in 1984, the Court again refused to add another exception and held that there can be no murder scene exception to the rule even if the search lasts two hours rather than four days.

To summarize, when a legal arrest is made on the premises, the officer or officers may, as an incident to the arrest, search the person of the defendant for weapons or evidence and, in addition, may search the area in which the defendant might reach to obtain a weapon or to destroy evidence. But a thorough search of the whole house as an incident to an arrest is not authorized on the "incident to arrest" grounds.

(4) Search of premises outside of buildings

Where the arrest is made outside of the residence or other building, the search of the person is authorized to protect the officer, and to prevent concealment or destruction of the evidence. In addition, the search may extend into the area into which the arrestee might reach. However, a search of outbuildings as an incident to the arrest would not be justified unless the contents came within the immediate reach of the arrestee.[14]

(5) Search of automobiles incidental to arrest

The discussion here concerns the search of an automobile as an incident to a lawful arrest, not a search under the so-called moving vehicle doctrine. The *Chimel* rule applies to automobiles just as it does to fixed premises; i.e., the arresting officer may search the person arrested and the immediate area in order to protect himself or to prevent the destruction or concealment of evidence.

The scope of the search of an automobile incident to a lawful arrest has been the topic of many lower court cases. For example, may the officer search the entire passenger compartment as an incident to the arrest when the arrest is made just outside the automobile? Can packages be opened that are found in the passenger compartment of the automobile when the search is incident to a lawful arrest? The U.S. Supreme Court answered some of these questions in 1981.[15]

In the *Belton* case, the Court established what has become known as the Belton Rule. In this case, an automobile in which the respondent was one of the occupants was stopped by a New York state policeman for traveling at an excessive rate of speed. After stopping the car, the officer smelled marijuana and saw, on the floor of the car, an envelope suspected of containing marijuana. He directed the occupants of the car to get out of the car and arrested them for unlawful possession of marijuana. After searching each of the occupants, he searched the passenger compartment of the car where he found a jacket belonging to the respondent. He unzipped the pockets and discovered cocaine.

After the Appellate Court reversed the conviction, the U.S. Supreme Court ruled that the search was justified. Reiterating that it is essential that police officers have a familiar standard in determining the scope of the search, the United States Supreme Court made these comments:

> Accordingly, we hold that when a policeman has made a lawful custodial arrest of the occupant of an automobile, he may, as a contemporaneous incident of that arrest, search the passenger compartment of the automobile.

---

[14] *Vale v. Louisiana* , 399 U.S. 30, 26 L.Ed.2d 409, 90 S.Ct. 1969 (1970).
[15] *New York v. Belton*, 453 U.S. 454, 69 L.Ed.2d 768, 101 S.Ct. 2860 (1981).

As to the contents of the containers found in the passenger compartment, the court continued with this sentence:

> The police may also examine the contents of any containers found within the passenger compartment, for if the passenger compartment is within reach of the arrestees, so also will containers within it be within his reach.

The Belton Rule is that police may search the passenger compartment of the automobile as incident to the arrest and may examine the contents of any container found in the passenger compartment whether it be opened or closed. It does not justify a search of the trunk of the car as an incident to a lawful arrest.

§6.3   Search with a valid waiver

One of the favorite tools used by police officers when seeking evidence is the consent search. In accord with general principle which allows a person to waive his constitutional rights, the rights protected under the Fourth Amendment may be waived. However, this and other constitutional rights are considered to be waived only after careful evaluation and only after certain requirements have been complied with. As a rule of law, the courts have taken the approach that a person will be presumed not to have waived his rights. The burden of showing that the rights have been waived is on the prosecution.

To determine if rights have been waived, certain principles have been established by the courts. These principles will be discussed in the following paragraphs.

a.   The consent must be voluntary

To be constitutionally adequate, the consent must be given without force, duress or compulsion of any kind. Mere submission to authority or mere acquiescence is not the specific consent that is required.

On the other hand, the *Miranda* type of warning is not required to waive the rights in a search and seizure situation. The United States Supreme Court in upholding the consent search included this comment:

> We hold only that when the subject is not in custody and the state attempts to justify a search on the basis of his consent, the Fourth and Fourteenth Amendments require that it demonstrate that the

consent was in fact voluntarily given, and not the result of duress or coercion, express or implied. Voluntariness is a question of fact to be determined from all of the circumstances, and while the subject's knowledge of the right to refuse is a factor to be taken into account, the prosecution is not required to demonstrate such knowledge as a prerequisite to establishing voluntary consent.[16]

In determining if the consent to the search is in fact voluntary or is the product of duress or coercion, the courts consider the "totality of circumstances."[17] In the *Mendenhall* case, officers told the suspect that she had a right to decline the search if she desired and she responded "go ahead." The court held that this was consent under the circumstances. However, one lower court cautioned that "only exceptionally clear evidence of consent should overcome a presumption that a person requested to accompany an agent to an office no longer would feel free to leave, and that silently following an officer would rarely constitute sufficient evidence of consent."[18]

What if the officer obtains consent by claiming that he has a search warrant that he will execute if the person in charge of the premises does not consent? If the officer does have a search warrant or if he indicates that he will apply for a search warrant, this is apparently not considered coercive.[19] This should be distinguished, however, from the situation where the officer claims he has a warrant and will use it if consent to search is not given when, in fact, he does not have a warrant, or has a warrant that is unserviceable.[20]

To avoid the risk of later challenge, the officer should not even comment concerning the search warrant unless he has a search warrant in his possession. In such case, it is preferable to proceed under the warrant rather than under the waiver.

---

[16] *Schneckloth v. Bustamonte*, U.S. 218, 36 L.Ed.2d 854, 93 S.Ct. 2041 (1973).

[17] *United States v. Mendenhall*, 446 U.S. 544, 64 L.Ed.2d 497, 100 S.Ct. 1870 (1980).

[18] *United States v. Berry*, 670 F 2d 583 (5th Cir. 1982).

[19] *United States v. Faruolo*, 506 F.2d 490 (2d Cir. 1974).

[20] *Middleton v. Commonwealth*, 502 S.W.2d 517 (Ky. 1973). *Bumper v. North Carolina* 391 U.S. 543, 20 L.Ed.2d 797, 88 S.Ct. 1788 (1968).

b.   The extensiveness of the search is limited to the exact words or meaning of consent

The consent to search must be such that it is clear that the person intends to give consent. Consent should be in specific terms. However, the courts have recognized a waiver where the meaning is clear. For example, if the consentor makes such comment as, "Come with me and I will show you where the stolen property may be found," the consent is valid. The officer who makes the search must carefully observe any geographic limitations placed upon the consent either directly or by inference. Therefore, a consent to search one portion of the premises is not a consent to search the other portions.

A second limitation concerns the items that can be seized. For example, a consent by the resident for the officers to search his house for narcotics does not authorize seizure of other articles such as ledgers. Other articles may be seized under the plain view doctrine that will be discussed later, but they can not be seized under the consent exception.[21]

c.   Consent may be withdrawn

One danger of making the search under the consent rule is that the consentor may withdraw this consent at any time. If the consentor does withdraw the consent during the process of the search, the officer must honor this right and stop the search immediately.[22] Under these circumstances, the officer may use any evidence he has obtained up to this point, or he may seize other evidence within view if the circumstances justify.

d.   The person giving the consent must have the capacity to do so

The most serious problem confronting the officer who is contemplating the consent search is whether the person who gives the consent is legally qualified to do so. This situation arises in the case of landlords, joint tenants, partners, spouses, or agents. The general rule as established by the United States Supreme Court is that, "The consent of one who possesses common authority over the premises or effects is valid against the absent non-consenting person with whom the authority is shared."[23]

---

[21]   *United States v. Dichiarinte*, 445 F.2d 126 (7th Cir. 1971).

[22]   *Strong v. United States*, 46 F.2d 257 (1st Cir. 1931).

[23]   *United States v. Matlock*, 415 U.S. 164, 39 L.Ed.2d 242, 94 S.Ct. 988 (1974).

Under this rule, a valid consent to search the premises may be given by a person who has immediate and present right to possess those premises. This third party consent does not rest upon the law of property but upon the reasonableness of recognizing that the absent party assumes a risk that a co-occupant might permit a search.[24]

(1) Consent by the spouse

Although there are some courts holding to the contrary, the modern rule is that the wife is in the position of a tenant-in-common and can consent to the search of premises occupied by both spouses.[25] In this situation, the wife does not waive the rights of her husband, but the consent is based on the principle that she has joint control of the premises and has the option of waiving her right to privacy therein. Under this view, it does not make any difference if the woman is the occupant's legal wife or not if she has the right to use and occupy the premises equal to that which a legal wife would have.[26]

Although it would seem that the general rule is that a spouse may not validly waive consent if the other spouse is occupying the premises at the time and refuses to authorize the search, one court has held that a person who shares living space with others can authorize police to search the residence even over the objection of the other inhabitant.[27] Also, the courts are generally in agreement that one spouse cannot consent to a search of a part of the premises used exclusively by the other spouse.

As to the latter point, one court rendered a decision which condemned the search of a rented garage which was leased entirely by the husband and not used at all by the wife who gave the consent.[28] But if the wife has access to a dresser drawer used by the husband, located in the room that is available to both, the wife's consent to take evidence from the dresser drawer is probably valid unless the facts indicate that one spouse has exclusive control over a portion of the premises or a particular container.[29] The same reasoning applies if the husband consents and evidence is used against the wife.

---

[24] *Coolidge v. New Hampshire*, 403 U.S. 443, 29 L.Ed.2d 564, 91 S.Ct. 2022 (1971).

[25] *United States v. Thompson*, 421 F.2d 373 (5th Cir. 1970).

[26] *White v. United States*, 444 F.2d 724 (10th Cir. 1971).

[27] *People v. Cosme*, 397 N.E.2d 1319 (1979).

[28] United States ex rel. *Cabey v. Mazurkiewicz*, 312 F.Supp. 11 (E.D. Pa. 1969).

[29] *People v. Stacey*, 58 Ill.2d 83, 317 N.E.2d 24 (1974).

(2) Consent by a parent

The general rule is that a minor child's possessory right in a family home is only that which he derives from his parent, and that the parent may authorize a consent search valid against the child.[30] The majority rule is that if an adult child is paying rent and has a room of his own which is used exclusively by that child, the parent cannot generally consent. On the other hand, if the parent has common access to those parts of the home, he or she may consent to a search of the area occupied in common in the absence of the adult child.[31]

(3) Consent by a minor child

An officer cannot rely on the consent given by a minor child. First, it would be very difficult to prove that the child understood that he did not have to give consent and, second, the minor child's interests in the property is not that of a tenant-in-common. It would seem, however, that an adult child who has the status of a joint tenant or resident does have the authority to consent to the search of the jointly used area.

(4) Consent to search for and seize articles left in another's care

If a person leaves articles in another's home or in another's care, the person who has custody of such articles may consent to their search of that article. If, for example, a borrower of a car has legitimate possession and control of that vehicle, the owner cannot complain if the borrower consents to a search of the car unless the owner has specifically told him in the beginning that he could not give such consent.[32]

As the burden of proof is on the prosecution to show that the consent was voluntary, this consent should be obtained in writing when possible, and should be witnessed by more than one person. If forms are used, they should be readily available at all times.

§6.4   Search of movable vehicles and objects

The Supreme Court of the United States has recognized a necessary difference between the search of a dwelling house, for which a warrant may

---

[30] *United States v. Peterson*, 524 F.2d 167 (4th Cir. 1975).

[31] *People v. Bunker*, 22 Mich. App. 396, 177 N.W.2d 644 (1970).

[32] *Marshall v. United States*, 352 F.2d 1013 (9th Cir. 1965).

be readily obtainable, and a search of a ship, boat, wagon, airplane, automobile, or other movable vehicle where it is not practical to secure a warrant because the object may be quickly moved out of the jurisdiction.[33] In 1970 the Supreme Court approved in the *Chambers* case the "moving vehicle doctrine" and reaffirmed the right of the officers to search a vehicle which is moving or about to be moved out of the jurisdiction, provided that there is probable cause to believe that the vehicle contains articles the officers are entitled to seize.[34] In *Chambers*, the Supreme Court referred to the earlier *Carroll* case and made the determination that the search warrant is unnecessary where there is probable cause to search an automobile stopped on the highway, the car is movable, the occupants are alerted, and the car's contents may never be found if a warrant must first be obtained. Under such circumstances, an immediate search is constitutionally permissible without a warrant. This doctrine applies even if the car has been driven by an officer to the station and time was available to secure a warrant.[35]

The justification for this exception is that because the vehicle is moving or about to be moved from the officer's jurisdiction, there is no time to get a search warrant even if probable cause for the warrant exists. Therefore these three requirements must be met if the search is to be justified under this exception: (1) the officer must have probable cause which would have justified a search warrant if one could have been obtained, (2) the vehicle must be moving or about to be moved, and (3) the facts must indicate that a warrant may not be readily obtained. The officer must at least have facts or information which would guarantee the authorization and issuance of a search warrant had an application been made. The difference is that probable cause is proved in court *after* the search rather than before a magistrate and before the search. This same rationale is applied when the search is made of a boat, plane, truck, trailer, mobile home, or tractor-trailer.[36]

In recent years, lower courts have been applying the so-called Carroll-Chambers doctrine to other movable objects. For example, the California Supreme Court found a degree of similarity between a motor vehicle and a package being sent by air freight. The Court concluded that the exception to the warrant requirements explained in *Chambers* applies to such a package.[37] And the Eighth Circuit Court had no difficulty in applying the rationale to the search of a duffel bag when probable cause existed and the item was

---

[33]   *Carroll v. United States*, 267 U.S. 132, 69 L.Ed. 543, 45 S.Ct. 280 (1925).

[34]   *Chambers v. Maroney*, 499 U.S. 42, 26 L.Ed.2d 419, 90 S.Ct. 1975 (1970).

[35]   *Texas v. White*, 423 U.S. 67, 46 L.Ed.2d 209, 96 S.Ct. 304 (1975).

[36]   *United States v. Bozada*, 473 F.2d 389 (8th Cir. 1973).

[37]   *People v. McKinnon*, 7 Cal.3d 399, 103 Cal. Rptr. 897, 500 P.2d 1097 (1972).

about to be moved.[38] In other cases, both federal and state courts have approved searches of suitcases in transit where exigent circumstances justify such action.[39]

In 1982 the United States Supreme Court rendered a decision which clarified the rule relating to containers found in an automobile. By a 6-3 vote, the United States Supreme Court concluded that police, acting under the automobile exception to the Fourth Amendment warrant requirement, may search every part of the vehicle, including closed containers that might conceal the contraband for which they are looking.[40] In the *Ross* case, the Court held in effect that if an officer has probable cause to search an occupied vehicle for a particular type of evidence, for example, contraband or stolen goods, he is entitled to conduct a warrantless search of all compartments or closed containers within the vehicle in which the evidence sought may reasonably be found.

Explaining the rationale for the automobile exception, the Court noted:

> The scope of warrantless search based on probable cause is no narrower--and no broader--than the scope of a search authorized by a warrant supported by probable cause. Only the prior approval of the magistrate is waived; the search otherwise is as the magistrate could authorize.

Adding more light on the automobile exception search, the Supreme Court noted that a search of containers seized from the vehicle three days after the vehicle's search does not violate the Fourth Amendment.[41]

As interpreted by the Supreme Court, if the officer had probable cause to make the search at the time the car was stopped, he may conduct a warrantless search of the vehicle under the moving vehicle doctrine even if it has been taken into police custody and returned to the station.[42] The rationale for this non-contemporaneous search is that once the officer has probable cause to make a search under the moving vehicle doctrine, he may act as if a warrant had been obtained. The legality of the search does not depend on whether the car has been immobilized but on whether the probable cause existed at the time the car was originally stopped.

---

[38] *United States v. Wilson*, 524 F.2d 595 (8th Cir. 1975).

[39] *People v. McKinnon, supra* n.32; *United States v. Mehciz*, 437 F.2d 145 (9th Cir. 1971).

[40] *United States v. Ross* 456, U.S. 798, 72 L.Ed.2d 572, 102 S.Ct. 2157 (1982).

[41] *United States v. Johns*, 469 U.S. 478, 83 L.Ed.2d 890, 105 S.Ct. 881 (1985).

[42] *Michigan v. Thomas*, 458 U.S. 259, 73 L.Ed.2d 750, 102 S.Ct. 3079 (1982).

Does the moving vehicle exception apply to motor homes?   The Supreme Court considered the legality of the search of a motor home temporarily parked in a downtown parking lot in 1985.[43] In the *Carney* case, officers had probable cause to believe that marijuana was possessed for sale from a motor home parked in a downtown lot in San Diego. The California Supreme Court determined that the search of the motor home was unreasonable and that the motor vehicle exception to the warrant requirements did not apply because of the expectation of privacy of occupants of a motor home. But the Chief Justice, writing for the United States Supreme Court, concluded that privacy expectations are reduced in automobiles not only because some parts of the vehicle are open to plain view, but also because motor vehicles are heavily regulated. The majority reasoned that as the vehicle is readily mobile and there is a reduced expectation of privacy stemming from its use as a licensed motor vehicle subject to regulation, it may be searched if located in a place not regularly used for residential purposes. If the motor home is permanently parked in a space designed for such vehicles and is not readily moveable, it is a "home" protected by the Fourth Amendment.

§6.5   Seizure without a search (plain view)

The provisions of the Fourth Amendment and the provisions of the state constitutions protect persons against unreasonable *searches* and *seizures*. Therefore, where there is no search *required*, the constitutional guarantee is not applicable. In other words, if the officer is in a place where he has a right to be and recognizes contraband, instrumentalities of the crime, or other evidence that he has a right to seize, he may seize that evidence that is in his plain view. The Supreme Court has explained that the police are not required to close their eyes and need not walk out and leave the article where they saw it. Any other principle might lead to an absurd result and at times perhaps even defeat the ends of justice.[44]

The plain view or open view doctrine is quite simple. The rationale is that where there *is no search necessary, there is no need* for Constitutional protection against an illegal search.

However, there are two legal conditions that must be met before this doctrine will apply: (1) the officer must be lawfully present when he views the object, and (2) the officer must recognize that the article is contraband, illegally possessed, stolen property or otherwise subject to seizure.

---

[43] *California v. Carney*, 471 U.S. 386, 85 L.Ed.2d 406, 105 S.Ct. 2066 (1985).

[44] *Washington v. Chrisman*, 455 U.S. 1, 70 L.Ed.2d 778, 102 S.Ct. 812 (1982).

The officer may be lawfully present under many circumstances. He may be in a part of a business establishment that is open to the public. He may see something through an open door or window. He may be on the premises to conduct an investigation, or probably in the most common situations, he may be on the premises to execute a search warrant. In any event, he must come upon the article to be seized without making a search (open view).

But if the officer becomes a trespasser on the property which is under the protection of the Fourth Amendment, his action then amounts to an illegal search and seizure. He cannot use information so obtained to procure a warrant, nor can he seize the evidence without a warrant.

In the case of *Washington v. Chrisman*, the Supreme Court agreed that a police officer was properly in a position to observe contraband from a doorway when he accompanied a student to his room to obtain identification.[45] The court commented:

> The "plain view" exception to the Fourth Amendment warrant requirement permits a law enforcement officer to seize what clearly is incriminating evidence or contraband when it is discovered in the place where the officer has a right to be.

The second requirement--that the officer must recognize the article to be seized as contraband, illegally possessed property, stolen property, or otherwise subject to seizure--is somewhat more difficult to comply with. The general rule is that the officer must recognize the article to be seized without further search. In the case of *Texas v. Brown* in 1983, the Court, in clarifying past decisions, indicated that the officer need not "know" that certain items are contraband or incident to the crime before the seizure is justified under the plain view approach; all that is necessary is that he have "probable cause" to believe that the evidence is subject to seizure.[46]

In that case, the Court agreed that the officer possessed probable cause to believe that opaque green party balloons in the car occupied by the defendant were subject to seizure where the officer's experience led him to believe that narcotics were frequently packaged in such balloons.

However, in another case the same court indicated that the search was invalid where the police had only reasonable suspicion (less than probable cause) to believe that stereo equipment was stolen.[47] Here, the officer, who was on the property legally, had to move a turntable to check the serial numbers. This amounted to a "search" without probable cause.

---

[45] *United States v. McDaniel*, 154 F.Supp. 1 (D.C. Cir. 1957).

[46] *Texas v. Brown*, 460 U.S. 730, 75 L.Ed.2d 502, 103 S.Ct. 1535 (1983).

[47] *Arizona v. Hicks*, __U.S.__, 94 L.Ed.2d 347, 107 S.Ct. 1149 (1987).

Two other cases indicate the expanding use of the plain-view search in seizing evidence. Using this doctrine, the Supreme Court in 1986 announced that the officers were justified in seizing a gun observed under the seat of a car while attempting to get the vehicle identification number (VIN).[48] In this *Class* case, an officer, after stopping the car, attempted to see the VIN but was unable to do so because some papers obscured the area on the dashboard where the number was located. In attempting to see the number, the officer reached into the interior of the car to remove the papers. In doing so, he saw the handle of a gun protruding from underneath the driver's seat and seized the gun. The Supreme Court indicated that as the officer was in the vehicle legally to observe the VIN and saw the gun in plain view, he had the authority to seize it.

Does the use of field glasses or a flashlight make the observation of seizable goods a violation of the Fourth Amendment? The U.S. Supreme Court has been consistent in holding that the use of field glasses or a telescope does not amount to a trespass so as to make the viewing a search. Determining that the use of field glasses does not violate the Constitution, the Court made this comment:

> It is likewise beyond dispute that Maples' action in shining his flashlight to illuminate the interior of Brown's car trenched upon no right secured to the latter by the Fourth Amendment...The use of a search light is comparable to the use of marine glass or a field glass. It is not prohibited by the Constitution.[49]

Numerous other courts have agreed that the use of artificial means to illuminate a darkened area simply does not constitute a search, and thus triggers no Fourth Amendment protection.

§6.6   Search by a private individual

The constitutional prohibitions against unreasonable searches and seizures operate only against official action. Therefore, where evidence is seized by a private person even though seized unlawfully it may be used in evidence. A private person who unlawfully enters the premises of another may be subject to a civil suit or even criminal action, but this does not contaminate the evidence he makes available to authorities. Such a search and seizure is outside the scope of the constitutional protection. Obviously, however, should the court find that a law enforcement officer participated in the

---

[48] *New York v. Class*, 475 U.S. 106, 89 L.Ed.2d 81, 106 S.Ct. 960 (1986).

[49] *Texas v. Brown, supra.*

search or in any way had knowledge that the search was to be made, the evidence would not be admissible.[50]

In interpreting this exception to the warrant rule, the Supreme Court in 1984 agreed that employers of private freight carriers were not government agents and that seizure of white powdery substances from damaged baggage did not constitute a search within the meaning of the Fourth Amendment.[51] In this case, the private freight carrier employees found a package opened and suspected that it contained narcotics. The agents got in touch with DEA agents, who made a field test of the powdery substance and determined that it was contraband. The United States Supreme Court approved the use of the evidence even though the DEA agents had advised earlier that the carrier employees should be on the alert for narcotics.

However, action by school officials was held to be "state action" rendering the Fourth Amendment applicable where marijuana was seized from a high school student.[52] The Court compromised, however, in establishing standards to be applied and agreed that, although school officials were not private individuals but public officials for purposes of the Fourth Amendment, they would not be held to the same probable cause standards as law enforcement agents. The legality of the search of the student depends simply on the reasonableness under the circumstances of the search. In defining this, the Court commented:

> Under ordinary circumstances, the search of a student by a school official will be justified at its inception when there are *reasonable grounds for suspecting* the student has violated or is violating either the law or rules of the school.
> (Emphasis added)

An issue which is becoming more difficult as time passes is whether the exclusionary rule should apply to private security personnel, private contract police, private investigators, and railroad police. In determining if such personnel act as private citizens or officials, each case will have to be scrutinized. If personnel who make such investigations and seize property are licensed by the state, there is a good chance that such licensed personnel will be considered "official" and the exclusionary rule will apply.

---

[50] *Lustig v. United States*, 338 U.S. 74, 93 L.Ed. 1819, 69 S.Ct. 1372 (1949).

[51] *United States v. Jacobsen*, 466 U.S. 109, 80 L.Ed.2d 85, 104 S.Ct. 1652 (1984).

[52] *New Jersey v. T.L.O.*, 469 U.S. 325, 83 L.Ed.2d 720, 105 S.Ct. 733 (1985).

§6.7   Search of premises not protected by the Fourth Amendment (open fields)

Not all property is protected by the Fourth Amendment, and searches of such unprotected property will not be considered unreasonable. The Fourth Amendment and the provisions of the various state constitutions protect the right of the people to be secure in their persons, houses, papers, and effects. Other property is not protected under the Constitution, although it might be protected under the trespass laws.

The term "houses" has been interpreted very broadly to include any dwelling, whether it be a mansion, a small house, apartment, hotel room, or even a tent. The house is protected even if it is temporarily occupied, as in the case of a summer or weekend home. However, once a dwelling has been vacated, as when a tenant checks out of a hotel, it is no longer protected.

The wording of the Constitution has been interpreted to protect places of business, effects such as automobiles, and the curtilage surrounding the home.[53] The curtilage has been defined as the open space situated within a common enclosure and belonging to the dwelling house. It is that place which is necessary and convenient and is habitually used for family purposes, including a yard, a garden, or even a field which is near to and used in connection with the dwelling.

Although the provisions of the Constitution have been applied broadly, some areas and certainly some effects are not protected. The best known exception is the "open fields." In one leading case, an area 50 to 100 yards from the defendant's residence was held to be open fields and not protected by the Constitution.[54] Other examples of areas not protected are a cave, a shack located a mile from any premises, and a field approximately 75 feet behind a house.

In more recent cases, the Supreme Court has rendered decisions which more accurately define what is included in the curtilage and has offered some guidelines in determining when the "open field" exception applies. After restating the open fields rationale, the Supreme Court in 1984 approved the seizure of marijuana which was located approximately one mile from the defendant's house.[55] In the *Oliver* case, officers drove past the defendant's house to a locked gate and along the road and found the marijuana field over a mile from the defendant's home. After the district court suppressed the evidence, the case was considered by the U.S. Supreme Court. The majority

---

[53]   *United States v. Rabinowitz*, 339 U.S. 56, 94 L.Ed. 653, 70 S.Ct. 430 (1950).
[54]   *Hester v. United States*, 265 U.S. 57, 68 L.Ed. 898, 44 S.Ct. 445 (1924).
[55]   *Oliver v. United States*, 466 U.S. 170, 80 L.Ed.2d 214, 104 S.Ct. 1735 (1984).

determined that the open field doctrine still applied and explained that this doctrine was founded upon the explicit language of the Fourth Amendment and that the special sanction accorded to persons, houses, papers and effects does not extend to open fields such as existed in this case.

Applying this reasoning, the Supreme Court in 1986 held that a 200-acre chemical plant operated by Dow Chemical Company was an open area of an industrial complex and more comparable to an open field. In that case, aerial photography of the chemical company's industrial complex was not a search for Fourth Amendment purposes.[56]

Reaffirming what the Court designated as the long-established doctrine that the Fourth Amendment protection against warrantless searches does not extend to "open fields," the majority of the Supreme Court also noted that a barn 60 yards from the house was not a part of the curtilage for Fourth Amendment purposes.[57] In the *Dunn* case, agents surreptitiously crossed several interior fences and approached the barn located 50 yards from the fence surrounding the family residence. From this vantage point and using a flashlight, they observed what appeared to be a drug laboratory and obtained a warrant to search the entire ranch.

The first reviewing court reversed the conviction of the defendant, reasoning that the barn was within the residence's curtilage and, therefore, within the Fourth Amendment protective ambit. In reversing the lower court and upholding the use of the evidence, the United States Supreme Court provided some guidelines. The Court indicated that the extent of curtilage questions should be resolved with particular reference to the following four factors: (1) the proximity of the area of the home, (2) whether the area is within an enclosure surrounding the home, (3) the nature and uses to which the area is put, and (4) the steps taken by the resident to protect the area from observation by passersby. Applying these four criteria, the court decided that the barn in this case was not within the curtilage and, therefore, not within the protective ambit of the Fourth Amendment.

This commonly called "open field" exception to the warrant requirement results from a legitimate interpretation of the scope of the Fourth Amendment. However, it should be kept in mind that even though the evidence might be admissible as an exception, the officer who enters private property could be trespassing if entry is prohibited by a statute of that state.

After a long debate by lower courts, the United States Supreme Court in 1988 concluded that the Fourth Amendment does not prohibit the warrantless search and seizure of garbage left for collection outside the curtilage of

---

[56] *Dow Chemical Co. v. United States*, __U.S.__, __L.Ed.2d__, 106 S.Ct. 1819 (1986).
[57] *United States v. Dunn*, __U.S.__, __L.Ed.2d__, 107 S.Ct. 1134 (1987).

the home.[58]   In this case, investigators obtained evidence of narcotics violations from garbage bags left on the curb in front of the defendant's house.
The majority first found that the curb was not part of the curtilage and, secondly, that residents of the house could have no reasonable expectation of
privacy in the inculpatory items which they discarded.   In regard to the expectation of privacy principle, the court resolved that:

> An expectation of privacy does not give rise to a Fourth Amend-
> ment protection, however, unless society is prepared to accept that
> expectation as objectively reasonable.

§6.8   Standing to challenge the search

The majority of the justices in the *Mapp* case indicated that the only
courtroom door remaining open to evidence secured by illegal search has
been closed.   Yet, evidence may be admitted, even if the search proves to be
in violation of the Fourth Amendment, if it is used against one who has no
standing to challenge the search.   As one court explained, "It is not enough
for a defendant to show that someone's constitutional rights have been violated; he must show that *his* own constitutional rights have been violated."[59]
Even though the person whose rights have been violated may complain and
in fact may bring civil action against the officers, the party who has no substantial possessory interest in the property or legitimate presence on the
premises cannot complain.

In the case of *Jones v. United States*,[60] the United States Supreme Court
restated its position that the person aggrieved by an unlawful search and
seizure must have been a victim of a search and seizure, but liberalized the
"standing requirements."   In that case, the Supreme Court held that one who
has possession of the premises, although he is not paying any rent, may challenge the seizure of goods on the premises.   However, where the defendant
has no proprietary or possessory interest in the premises and is not on the
premises, he cannot be heard to complain as he has no standing to object to
the admissibility of the evidence.   Some examples will clarify this rule.

In a Kentucky case the Court of Appeals held that the seizure of a revolver from the hallway of another's home in which the defendant did not

---

[58]   *California v. Greenwood*, __U.S.__, __L.Ed.2d__, 108 S.Ct. 1625 (1988).
See case for review of lower court decisions.

[59]   *Lopata v. State*, 118 MD.App. 451, 307 A.2d 721 (1973).

[60]   362 U.S. 257, 4 L.Ed.2d 697, 80 S.Ct. 725 (1960).

show any *property* rights or possessory interest was proper.[61] The United States Supreme Court of Appeals for the Sixth Circuit, although excluding evidence against the second co-conspirator, admitted the evidence against the second co-conspirator who had no interest whatsoever in the premises.[62] One paragraph from that case succinctly explains the reasoning for this exclusionary exception:

> Fourth Amendment rights are personal rights which, like some other constitutional rights, may not be vicariously asserted. In order to have standing to object to an unlawful search, a person must be the individual against whom the search was directed, and not merely one who is prejudiced through the use of evidence gathered in a search directed at someone else.

Does the "no standing to challenge" rule apply to stolen or misappropriated automobiles? According to the justices who decided the case of *Palmer v. State*, the overwhelming weight of authority and the better reasoning are represented by the cases which hold squarely that the thief has no standing in a stolen automobile.[63] The Court explained that no valuable social purpose could conceivably be served by extending the protection of the Fourth Amendment to a thief in a stolen automobile.

Likewise, this doctrine is legitimately applied where the automobile is misappropriated even if not actually stolen. For example, where the defendant obtained an automobile from a car rental corporation by misrepresentation, he committed "larceny by trick" and therefore did not have standing to object to the search of the automobile.[64]

The United States Supreme Court has strongly supported the "no standing" reasoning in holding that a passenger in an automobile cannot complain if an illegal search is made where he has neither a property nor possessory interest in the automobile searched nor an interest in the property seized.[65] Only those who have a constitutional standing can challenge the admissibility of the evidence.

---

[61] *Geary v. Commonwealth*, 503 S.W.2d 505 (Ky. 1972).

[62] *United States v. Hearn*, 496 F.2d 236 (6th Cir. 1974).

[63] *Palmer v. State*, 14 Md.App. 159, 286 A.2d 572 (1972). See cases cited in that case.

[64] *Shope v. State*, 18 Md.App. 472, 307 A.2d 730 (1973).

[65] *Rakes v. Illinois*, 439 U.S. 128, 58 L.Ed.2d 387, 99 S.Ct. 421 (1978).

Like reasoning was followed where the evidence of a crime was obtained from the home of one of the defendant's mother where the defendant was not living in the house and had no possessory rights.[66]

One additional comment before leaving the "standing to challenge" exception: where a defendant challenges the admissibility of physical evidence or makes a motion to suppress, he bears the ultimate burden of establishing standing to challenge the admissibility of such evidence.[67]

§6.9   Search after lawful impoundment (inventory searches)

Often the police officer has the duty and responsibility either by law or departmental regulation to impound a car that has been abandoned, is blocking traffic, is illegally parked, or is in the officer's care for some other reason. In such instances, the officer is often required to make an inventory of the contents of the vehicle before taking it to an impoundment lot. Generally, there is no legal prohibition concerning the use of evidence coming within his possession as a result of such inventory.

The rationale for the use of evidence obtained as a result of the "inventory search" is sound. The officer should not be required to close his eyes and not seize stolen or contraband evidence so disclosed. As in the case of other legal tools, however, some law enforcement officers have overused and abused this "inventory seizure," in many instances carrying the search far beyond that justified. As a result, as one court stated, there has been a yawning credibility gap wrought by inventory searches.[68]

The purpose of making an inventory of the contents of an impounded car is to safeguard the owner and protect the government against false claims of loss. This would not justify a search into those parts of the car that are not normally searched when making an inventory. For example, a search into the hubcaps or a search into the area under the dashboard would not be a legitimate inventory search. If, therefore, the police officer's conduct indicates that the detention is exploratory rather than an inventory, the use of the fruits of the search are forbidden.[69]

Partially as a result of the abuses, some state courts have prohibited an inventory search of the entire automobile. For example, the Kentucky Court

---

[66] *United States v. Salvucci*, 448 U.S. 83, 65 L.Ed.2d 619, 100 S.Ct. 2547 (1980).

[67] *People v. Berrios*, 28 N.Y.2d 361, 321 N.Y.S.2d 884, 270 N.E.2d 709 (1971).

[68] *Dixon v. State*, 23 Md.App. 19, 327 A.2d 516 (1974).

[69] *State v. Wallen*, 185 Neb. 44, 173 N.W.2d 372 (1970).

of Appeals agreed that officers may close and lock a car and seize whatever is in plain view in the process, but they may not open compartments and containers within the vehicle.[70] The Wisconsin Supreme Court, in suppressing evidence obtained after an inventory was made of an impounded car, acknowledged that cases from other jurisdictions are divided on the question of whether making an inventory of the contents of an impounded car is actually a search, but the Court concluded that protecting the police from false claims of theft or "safeguarding" the defendant's property does not justify an inspection of closed suitcases and containers.[71]

Because of the widely different opinions of lower courts concerning the seizure of articles from an impounded car, the United States Supreme Court in 1976 placed a limited stamp of approval on this procedure.[72] In the *Opperman* case, an automobile was towed to the city impound lot after it had been parked illegally overnight. From outside the car, the police officer observed a watch on the dashboard and some items of personal property located on the back seat of the car. At his direction, the car was unlocked and a standard inventory form was used to inventory the contents. Marijuana was found in the unlocked glove compartment. It was seized and used in evidence. After conviction in the lower court, the Supreme Court of South Dakota reversed the conviction, concluding that the evidence had been obtained in violation of the Fourth Amendment (as made applicable to the states by the Fourteenth Amendment).

The United States Supreme Court reversed the decision of the South Dakota Supreme Court and held that the evidence was properly admitted. The Court, in approving this procedure in limited circumstances, first distinguished between automobiles and homes or offices in relation to the Fourth Amendment protections, and then, under the facts of the individual case, approved the seizure of evidence from the impounded car. The majority pointed out that the police were indisputably engaged in a "caretaker" search of the lawfully impounded automobile and that there was no suggestion of investigatory motive on the part of the officers.

Citing the *Opperman* case, the Supreme Court in 1987 reaffirmed the use of evidence obtained during a lawful inventory of an automobile.[73] In the *Bertine* case, the officer arrested a driver for driving his van while under the influence of alcohol. After he was taken into custody and before a tow truck arrived to take the van to an impoundment lot, another officer, acting in ac-

---

[70]   *City of Danville v. Dawson*, 528 S.W.2d 687 (Ky. 1975).

[71]   *State v. McDougal*, 68 Wis.2d 399, 228 N.W.2d 671 (1975).

[72]   *South Dakota v. Opperman*, 428 U.S. 364, 49 L.Ed.2d 1000, 96 S.Ct. 3092 (1976).

[73]   *Colorado v. Bertine*, __U.S.__, 93 L.Ed.2d 739, 107 S.Ct. 738 (1987).

cordance with local police procedures, inventoried the van's contents, opening a closed backpack in which he found various containers holding controlled substances, cocaine paraphernalia, and a large amount of cash. The United States Supreme Court agreed with the prosecutor that there was no showing that the police acted in bad faith for the sole purpose of conducting an investigatory search. The majority of the court, in affirming the use of the evidence, emphasized the fact that the inventory search serves a governmental interest in protecting the owner's property while it is in police custody, insuring against claims of lost, stolen, or vandalized property, and guarding the police from danger.

Despite the cases to the contrary, the majority view is that evidence obtained during a legitimate inventory of a legally impounded car may be used in evidence. If the inventory search goes further than necessary to carry out the purposes of the inventory and is a mere subterfuge, then it is quite obvious that the evidence will be inadmissible. If there is continued abuse of this privilege, there is a good chance that either the Supreme Court or additional state courts will hold such evidence inadmissible or at least reduce the physical area of the inventory search.

§6.10   Stop and frisk seizures

If a suspect is stopped when there is no probable cause to make an arrest, and therefore no justifiable search incident to the arrest, may the officer nevertheless search (stop and frisk) the person whom he has detained? In previous chapters, the authority to detain where there is probable cause to arrest was fully discussed. The question that presents itself in relation to search and seizure is the extent to which the officer may seize weapons or evidence from the suspect under the stop and frisk authority.

Until the case of *Terry v. Ohio*[74] in 1968, there was considerable doubt as to whether a police officer could stop a suspicious person on the street, ask him questions, and then frisk the suspect for weapons. At least some of the doubt was removed in the *Terry* case. In *Terry*, a police officer stopped a suspect on a downtown Cleveland, Ohio street after the officer had observed the suspect and two other men "casing" a job. Without putting the suspect under arrest, the police officer patted down the outside clothing of the suspect for weapons and later removed a pistol from the suspect's overcoat pocket.

Admitting that there was no probable cause to make an arrest, the Supreme Court was faced with two questions. First, did the officer have the authority to detain, and second, did the officer have the authority to frisk a

---

[74]   392 U.S. 1, 20 L.Ed.2d 889, 88 S.Ct. 1868 (1968).

detained suspect for weapons? The Court was careful to distinguish this stop and frisk from the searches incidental to a lawful arrest, explaining:

> The sole justification for the search in the present situation is the protection of the police officer and others nearby, and must therefore be confined in scope to an intrusion reasonably designed to discover guns, knives, clubs, or other hidden instruments for the assault of the police officer.

It is emphasized that the frisk authorized in the detention situation is only for the protection of the officer and is limited to patting down rather than a full-scale search. However, this "frisk" authorization did not extend to an officer who, while patting down a suspect, found a small package of narcotics.[75] The Court explained that while there is a self-protective search for weapons, the officer must be able to point to particular facts from which he reasonably inferred that the individual was armed and dangerous.

The officer must be aware of the difference between a full search incidental to a lawful arrest and a "frisk for weapons" predicated on a frisk after a detention. As was pointed out in the *Chimel* case discussed earlier, when the search is made incidental to a lawful arrest, the person of the arrestee and the immediate area may be searched for weapons and evidence which may be destroyed or concealed. However, where the officer does not have an arrest warrant nor sufficient reasonable grounds for an arrest, but does have sufficient evidence to detain as provided in the *Terry* rule, he may pat down the outer clothing only for *weapons* and/or *means of escape*. If the officer discovers evidence or obtains information which will give him probable cause or reasonable grounds to arrest, he then may place the suspect under arrest and make a full-scale search.

As was inevitable, the lower courts have been called upon to interpret further the extent of the seizure under the Terry rule. One question left unanswered by *Terry* was whether the article which did not feel like a knife or club could be a dangerous weapon and therefore subject to seizure. A second question was whether the officer, while in the process of seizing the weapon, could legally seize other articles which were not considered dangerous to the officer. According to the California Supreme Court, an officer may pat down a suspect for atypical weapons if the officer can articulate facts which reasonably support a suspicion that the particular suspect is armed with a weapon such as a "sap."[76] This would indicate that if the officer can articulate facts which reasonably lead him to believe that the person he has

---

[75] *Sibron v. New York*, 392 U.S. 40, 20 L.Ed.2d 917, 88 S.Ct. 1889 (1968).
[76] *People v. Collins*, 1 Cal.3d 658, 83 Cal.Rptr. 179, 463 P.2d 403 (1970).

stopped carries razor blades, brass knuckles, or other atypical weapons peculiar to the area, he can reasonably pat down the suspect and seize such weapons.

As to the authority of the officer to seize evidence other than weapons obtained while checking the suspect in a stop and frisk situation, it is apparent that the seizure without a search rule applies. If the officer, in order to protect himself, reaches into a suspect's pocket to obtain a weapon, but in addition to, or instead of, a weapon, he finds other contraband, the use of such contraband as evidence is legitimate.[77] As an example, the Fourth Circuit Court approved the seizure of cocaine which came into the view of the officer after he had detained a suspect and checked a zipper bag for weapons.[78] In the opinion of the majority of the justices of the Fourth Circuit Court, the seizure of narcotics did not depend for its validity upon probable cause for arrest but was justified by the guidelines for protective searches established by *Terry v. Ohio.*

From the foregoing it can be concluded that the officer, under the proper circumstances, may frisk for weapons a person who has been detained. If such weapons are found, they may be used in evidence. Also, some courts have approved the use of evidence other than weapons when such evidence comes within the possession of the officer during a legitimate pat down for weapons.

In the *Terry* case, the Court approved the frisk of a pedestrian. Following the case, the courts were requested to consider if a *Terry*-type frisk could be made of occupants of a car following the issuance of a traffic citation. In the case of *Pennsylvania v. Mimms*, police officers stopped a vehicle with an expired license plate for the purpose of issuing a traffic summons.[79] When the driver stepped out of the car, the officer noticed a large bulge under the motorist's jacket and, fearing that the bulge might be a weapon, frisked the motorist and discovered a .38 caliber loaded revolver. The Pennsylvania Supreme Court reversed the conviction for carrying a concealed weapon, finding that the revolver was seized contrary to the guarantees found in the Fourth Amendment. The majority of the Supreme Court, however, explained that such a frisk is not unreasonable, commenting:

> We think it too plain for argument that the state's proffered justification--the safety of the officer--is both legitimate and weighty. Certainly it would be unreasonable to require that police officers take unnecessary risks in the performance of their duties.

---

[77] *People v. Woods*, 6 Cal.App.3d 832, 86 Cal.Rptr. 264 (1970).

[78] *United States v. Poms*, 484 F.2d 919 (4th Cir. 1974).

[79] *Pennsylvania v. Mimms*, 434 U.S. 106, 54 L.Ed.2d 331, 98 S.Ct. 330 (1977).

The next issue considered by the Supreme Court was whether a passenger compartment of a car may be frisked under the Terry doctrine where there is no probable cause to make a search incidental to the lawful arrest. In an opinion written by Justice O'Connor, the majority of the Supreme Court approved the seizure of weapons from the passenger compartment of an automobile when the driver of the car walked toward the car after a police officer arrived at the scene.[80] Shining his flashlight into the car, the officer saw something under the arm rest, and upon lifting the arm rest, saw an open pouch that contained what appeared to be marijuana. The Court agreed that the protective search of the passenger compartment was reasonable under the principle articulated in *Terry*.

From this and other cases it can be concluded that if an officer stops a car to issue a traffic citation, he may, for his protection, order the driver to step out of the car, and if the facts available warrant a man of reasonable caution to conclude the person is armed and poses a serious and present danger to the safety of the officer, a pat down or frisk for weapons is justified. Also, if the officer can articulate reasons for believing a present danger exists, he may search the passenger compartment of the car for weapons. If, during the search of the passenger compartment for weapons to protect himself, the officer comes upon contraband or illegally possessed evidence, he may seize that evidence under the "seizure without a search" principle.

The third *Terry* issue is whether luggage may be temporarily detained on suspicion amounting to less than probable cause. In the case of *United States v. Place*, the majority of the Supreme Court found that if an officer's observations lead him reasonably to believe that a traveler is carrying luggage that contains narcotics, then the officer may detain the luggage briefly to investigate the circumstances that aroused his suspicion, providing the investigative detention is properly limited in scope.[81] Although providing that luggage may be detained under certain circumstances, the Court in the *Place* case noted that a detention of 90 minutes between the seizure of the luggage and a sniff test by a trained narcotics dog was too long.

The effect of the *Place* case, however, appears to make the *Terry* principles applicable to detention of luggage for further investigation if the officer can demonstrate reasonable, articulable suspicion premised on objective facts that the luggage contained contraband or evidence of a crime.

The Supreme Court's approval of the *Terry*-type stop and frisk has been very helpful to police officers in carrying out their responsibilities. If this

---

[80] *Michigan v. Long*, 463 U.S. 1032, 77 L.Ed.2d 1201, 103 S.Ct. 3469 (1983).

[81] *United States v. Place*, 462 U.S. 696, 77 L.Ed.2d 110, 103 S.Ct. 2637 (1983).

practice is to continue to receive court approval, however, the officer must constantly be cautious that he does not overstep the line and use the procedure as a subterfuge for making an illegal search.

§6.11   Search of pervasively regulated business

Do pervasively regulated businesses such as those licensed to sell alcoholic beverages or licensed under the gun control act to sell firearms have the same constitutional protections as others? Depending upon the statutes and ordinances, these businesses may not have the same protection. For example, in the case of *United States v. Biswell*, a Treasury agent, acting under the authority of the Gun Control Act of 1968, requested entry into a locked gun storeroom and was admitted after showing the owner the provisions of the statute.[82] The Gun Control Act authorizes entry into the premises during business hours for purposes of inspecting or examining records and documents required to be kept on firearms or ammunition stored by the dealer at such premises. The Supreme Court reversed the holding of intermediate courts and approved the seizure of illegally possessed firearms, explaining that close scrutiny of the traffic in firearms is justified and that this limited threat to the dealer's expectations of privacy is reasonable. The majority explained:

> When a dealer chooses to engage in this type of pervasively regulated business and to accept a federal license, he does so with the knowledge that his business records, firearms, and ammunition will be subject to effective inspection.

Courts have applied the same reasoning to licensed dealers in alcoholic beverage, explaining that the dealer waives certain rights when he obtains the license.[83] Before any action is taken to search such a place of business or to seize evidence therefrom, the officer must check all statutes and ordinances to be sure that he has this right. Probably a better practice would be to check with the county attorney or legal advisor to determine the limits on the authority.

---

[82]   406 U.S. 311, 32 L.Ed.2d 87, 92 S.Ct. 1593 (1972).

[83]   *Colonnade Catering Corp. v. United States*, 397 U.S. 72, 25 L.Ed.2d 60, 90 S.Ct. 774 (1970).

§6.12   Seizure of verbal evidence via concealed recorders or microphones

In the case of *On Lee v. United States*, an undercover federal narcotics agent, wearing a small microphone and an antenna concealed in his overcoat, entered the laundry of an old acquaintance.[84]   Unknown to the suspect, a second narcotics agent was stationed outside with a radio receiver tuned in on that conversation. At the trial, the second agent was permitted to testify as to matters overheard. This procedure was challenged on the ground that it was an illegal search and seizure in violation of the Fourth Amendment. Two questions were presented in this factual situation. One, does the seizure of verbal evidence by way of a microphone or a recorder come within the purview of the Fourth Amendment?   Two, if words as well as tangible evidence are protected by the Fourth Amendment, did the conduct of the officers violate established search and seizure standards as established by the Supreme Court?

A series of cases decided by the Supreme Court leaves no doubt that the Court considers eavesdropping by electronic devices or bugging to fall within the ambit of the Fourth Amendment.[85]   Therefore, all of the amendments' safeguards which apply to the seizure of tangible goods also apply to the "seizure" of verbal evidence.

On the other hand, the courts have been consistent in holding that there is no federal constitutional objection to the use of electronic recording or transmitting conversations with others, whether accomplished by police agent or informant, if one party to the conversation is aware and agrees to the recording.[86] In the *White* case, the suspect was convicted of violation of the narcotics laws. At the trial, evidence of incriminating statements made by the defendant and recorded by government agents was admitted. A government informant had consented to the agent's fixing a transmitter on the informant's person as he talked with the defendant. One agent, with the informant's consent, was in the kitchen closet and heard the conversation. The second agent was outside the house using a radio receiver which recorded the conversation. Although the prosecution was unable to locate and produce the informant at trial, the trial accepted the testimony of the two agents.

---

[84]   343 U.S. 747, 96 L.Ed. 1270, 72 S.Ct. 967 (1952).

[85]   *Katz v. United States*, 389 U.S. 347, 19 L.Ed. 576, 88 S.Ct. 507 (1967) and *Berger v. New York*, 388 U.S. 41, 18 L.Ed.2d 1040, 87 S.Ct. 1873 (1967).

[86]   *Lopez v. United States*, 373 U.S. 427, 10 L.Ed.2d 462, 83 S.Ct. 1381 (1963); *Osborn v. United States*, 385 U.S. 323, 17 L.Ed.2d 394, 87 S.Ct. 429 (1966); *United States v. White*, 401 U.S. 745, 28 L.Ed.2d 453, 91 S.Ct. 1122 (1971).

The defendant was found guilty in the lower court, but the Circuit Court of Appeals held that the agent's testimony was inadmissible under the Fourth Amendment, and reversed the conviction of the lower court. However, Mr. Justice White, speaking for the United States Supreme Court majority, concluded that the procedure did not violate the Fourth Amendment and reversed the Circuit Court of Appeals. In explaining the reason for such a holding, the Supreme Court stated:

> For constitutional purposes, no different result is required if the agent, instead of immediately reporting and transcribing his conversations with the defendant, either (1) simultaneously records them with electronic equipment which he is carrying on his person or (2) carries radio equipment which simultaneously transmits the conversations either to recording equipment located elsewhere or to the other agents monitoring the transmitting frequency.

In 1979 the United States Supreme Court again affirmed the rule that consensual monitoring and recording by means of a transmitter concealed on an informant's person is not a violation of the Fourth Amendment even though the defendant did not know that he was speaking with a government agent.[87] The Court went even further by stating that evidence so acquired is permissible even if obtained in violation of the Internal Revenue Service regulations which prohibit such recordings unless approved by certain named authorities in the Internal Revenue Service. As the Internal Revenue agents acted in good faith in permitting eavesdropping, neither the violation of the rule nor the electronic eavesdropping itself violated due process, equal protection, or the Fourth Amendment.[88]

Even if there is no constitutional objection to the use of electronic surveillance equipment when one party consents, and there is no objection to this under federal law, a state statute or constitutional provision may prohibit this use.[89] It is therefore essential that the state wiretapping and eavesdrop-

---

[87] *United States v. Caceres*, 440 U.S. 741, 59 L.Ed.2d 733, 99 S.Ct. 1465 (1979).

[88] For a comprehensive discussion of the use of eavesdropping and wiretapping, see Chapter 5, *Constitutional Law*, Klotter and Kanovitz, 5th Ed., Anderson Publishing Co.

[89] *People v. Beavers*, 393 Mich. 554, 227 N.W.2d 511 (1975). Electronic surveillance where the officer is not present, or where neither party has consented to the listening, is regulated by federal law at 18 U.S.C. §§ 2510-2520.

ping laws be consulted and interpreted before such devices or techniques are used.

§6.13   Summary

Although there are no provisions in the Fourth Amendment authorizing a search without a warrant, the courts have affirmed that it was not the intention of the framers of the Constitution to condemn all warrantless searches. However, if the search cannot be made under a warrant or one of the recognized exceptions, it is very likely that evidence seized will not be admitted.

Very early, the courts authorized a search without a warrant when it was made incidental to a lawful arrest. In order for such a search to be legal and the evidence admissible, the arrest must be lawful and the search must be contemporaneous with the arrest. Under the most recent Supreme Court cases, if a person is lawfully arrested, his person may be searched and articles on his person seized even though the articles are not connected with the crime. Also, the search may extend to the area within his reach for weapons or evidence which might be destroyed or concealed.

A person may waive the rights that are guaranteed by the Fourth Amendment if he does so voluntarily and freely. There are some dangers, however, in relying upon the consent search. First, the search is limited to the exact words or meaning of the consent. Second, the consent may be withdrawn by the consentor. Third, the person giving the consent must have the legal capacity to do so.

The third warrantless search authorized by the courts is the search of movable vehicles and objects. In approving this exception, the courts have recognized that it is often impossible to obtain warrants for objects which may be moved from the jurisdiction. In such a case, the search may nevertheless be made if there is probable cause which would have justified the issuance of a search warrant, if the vehicle or article is moving or about to be moved, and if the facts indicate that a warrant may not readily be obtained.

As the Constitution protects against unreasonable searches and seizures, a seizure of articles does not violate that Constitution where there is no search. For this "plain view" exception to apply, the officer must be lawfully present on the premises when he views the object and must have probable cause to believe that the article is contraband, illegally possessed, or otherwise subject to seizure.

As the constitutional prohibitions operate only against official action, evidence seized by a private person without the knowledge or acquiescence of an official may be used in evidence even if the search would have been illegal otherwise. Also, the constitutional provisions of the Fourth Amendment relate only to persons, houses, papers, and effects. Other property is not protected under the Constitution. Hence, the search of property not protected, such as open fields, is not in violation of the Fourth Amendment, and the evidence will probably be admissible.

Only a person whose rights are violated may challenge the illegal search. The defendant who has no proprietary or possessory interest in the premises and is not on the premises may not be heard to complain.

The general rule is that an officer who is legitimately conducting an inventory search of a lawfully impounded car may use the evidence coming within his possession as a result of such inventory. This is merely an extension in the seizure without a search exception. Largely because the impoundment search has been abused, there has resulted a yawning credibility gap according to the opinion of some justices. In some states, the officer may only close the car doors and impound the car without making a further search.

Even though the officer sometimes has no probable cause to make an arrest, he could have the authority to stop and frisk a suspect. Where the sole justification of the frisk is to protect the officer and others nearby, the officer may pat down the outer clothing and seize guns, knives, clubs, or other hidden instruments which might be used to assault the police officer. This evidence may be used in court. There is some legal justification for seizing evidence other than weapons when this other evidence comes within the view or possession of the officer while he is legitimately seizing or searching for weapons.

Although words as well as tangible evidence are protected by the Fourth Amendment, there is no federal constitutional objection to the electronic recording or transmitting of conversations with others if one party to the conversation is aware of and agrees to the recording procedure. The rationale is that a person who voluntarily converses with another assumes the risk that the other will report or later transcribe the conversation. For constitutional purposes, there is no different result if the agent, instead of immediately reporting and transcribing the conversation with the defendant, records or transmits the conversation by means of electronic equipment.

Chapter 7

QUESTIONING SUSPECTS

In dealing with statements obtained through interrogation, we do not purport to find all confessions inadmissible. Confessions remain a proper element in law enforcement. Any statement given freely and voluntarily without any compelling influences is, of course, admissible in evidence.

Miranda v. Arizona,
384 U.S. 436, 16 L.Ed.2d 694,
86 S.Ct. 1602 (1966)

Section
7.1   General considerations
7.2   The free and voluntary rule
7.3   The delay in arraignment rule
7.4   Warning and waiver requirements (*Miranda* rule)
7.5   Exclusion of confession as a means of enforcing
       the Fourth Amendment
7.6   Right to counsel
7.7   Corroboration
7.8   Derivative evidence
7.9   Admissible statements (including "good faith" exception)
7.10   Admissibility of a second confession after an
       inadmissible first confession
7.11   Summary

§7.1 General considerations

Every police officer, from the officer who makes the initial detention and arrest to the investigator, must be familiar with the rules relating to questioning suspects. Improper questioning initially may not only contaminate the statements obtained but contaminate evidence located as a result of the improper questioning. This does not mean that all questioning is improper. The United States Supreme Court in the case of *Miranda v. Arizona* pointed out that that decision was not intended to hamper the traditional functions of police officers in investigating crime. The Court specifically approved inquiry of persons not under restraint, general on-the-scene questioning as to facts surrounding the crime, and other general questioning of citizens in the fact-finding process.[1] The use of questions in ferreting out the guilty is a proper and necessary tool in protecting society.

What the Court has condemned and continues to condemn is the improper use of questioning, or using questioning as a substitute for a thorough investigation. The officer who is familiar with the rules relating to questioning can determine when it is preferable to question the suspect and when it is advisable to remain silent. Questioning is only one technique in solving a crime and should be utilized only when that technique has been determined to be preferable after considering other investigative techniques.

Before a confession may be admissible as evidence for most purposes, it must pass at least five tests. First, a confession must be given freely and voluntarily. Second, a confession must meet those requirements established by the United States Supreme Court in the *McNabb* and *Mallory* cases, or the so-called "delay in arraignment" requirements. Third, with some exceptions, a confession will not be admitted if the *Miranda* warnings are not given. Fourth, a confession is not admissible if it is tainted by an illegal arrest or an illegal search. And fifth, a confession may be inadmissible if there is failure to provide the suspect with counsel. In addition, independent corroborative evidence must be introduced. These various tests or hurdles will be discussed in the following sections.

§7.2 The free and voluntary rule

The traditional test to determine the admissibility of a confession is known as the free and voluntary rule.

---

[1] *Miranda v. Arizona*, 384 U.S. 436, 16 L.Ed.2d 694, 86 S.Ct. 1602 (1966).

Although the free and voluntary rule has been in effect throughout the history of this country, the scope of the rule has been broadened in recent years. This rule was developed in England and in the United States and was applied in the courts in this country at the time of the adoption of the Constitution. The rule merely states that a confession of a person accused of crime is admissible in evidence against the accused only if it was freely and voluntarily made, i.e., made without duress, fear, or compulsion in its inducement and with the suspect's full knowledge of the nature and consequence of the confession.[2]

If a confession is not voluntary, it cannot be relied upon as trustworthy. Also, the Supreme Court has determined that if the confession is not freely and voluntarily given, it violates the self-incrimination clause of the Fifth Amendment.[3]

If actual force is used, even though slight, the courts will consider the confession inadmissible. Also, threats of force will make the confession inadmissible. For example, threatening a suspect by telling him that a mob outside the jail "is going to get him" is sufficient to make the confession involuntary.[4] In addition to force and threats of force, psychological coercion may be considered sufficient to make a confession involuntary. For example, a threat by a police officer to "bring the accused's invalid wife to police headquarters" prompted the accused to confess to murder and was subsequent grounds for reversal.[5]

Today, most of the statements obtained are challenged not because force or duress is used but because they are obtained by psychological methods which have been condemned by the courts. For example, the Eighth Circuit Court of Appeals determined that the confession of a handcuffed murder defendant who had been questioned about twenty-five times, while without nourishment, in a small, hot room in the presence of six officers, was involuntary.[6]

Any force, threats of force, or other coercion which would be likely to cause a person to make a statement he would not otherwise make may render a confession involuntary and inadmissible.

What degree of proof is necessary in determining the voluntariness of a confession? Must the confession be found by the jury to be voluntary beyond a reasonable doubt or voluntary by the preponderance of the evidence? Af-

---

[2]   *People v. Fox*, 319 Ill. 606, 150 N.E. 347 (1926).

[3]   *Bram v. United States*, 168 U.S. 532, 42 L.Ed. 568, 18 S.Ct. 183 (1897).
       Miller v. Fenton, 474 U.S. 104, 88 L.Ed.2d 405, 106 S.Ct. 5156 (1985).

[4]   *Payne v. Arkansas*, 356 U.S. 560, 2 L.Ed.2d 975, 78 S.Ct. 844 (1958).

[5]   *Rogers v. Richmond*, 365 U.S. 534, 5 L.Ed.2d 760, 81 S.Ct. 735 (1961).

[6]   *Stidham v. Swenson*, 506 F.2d 478 (8th Cir. 1974).

ter years of doubt, the Supreme Court in 1972 determined that the Constitution required only the "preponderance of the evidence" test. This means that the weight of the evidence must show that the confession is voluntary, but it is not necessary to show that the confession is voluntary beyond a reasonable doubt.[7]

§7.3 The delay in arraignment rule

Some statements are challenged because they were obtained "prior to arraignment," even though they are admittedly freely and voluntarily made. If the officer "unnecessarily" delays taking the person apprehended before a judicial officer as required by state or federal law, a confession or statement made during the delay probably will not be admitted. This rule was first announced in 1943 in the case of *McNabb v. United States*.[8] There, federal officers obtained a confession from suspects who were held for several days without being taken before a magistrate. The Supreme Court, in reversing the conviction, based its holding purely on the ground that evidence was secured in disregard of the federal statutory procedures established by Congress.

The delay in arraignment rule was revived and reemphasized in a case that received national recognition. In the case of *Mallory v. United States*,[9] the defendant was apprehended between 2:00 p.m. and 2:30 p.m. the day following a rape in Washington, D.C. Rather than taking the arrestee before a commissioner as required by federal law, the suspect was questioned until about 8:00 p.m., when he first admitted some part in the crime. The commissioner could not be located that evening and the suspect was not taken before the commissioner until the following morning. In reversing the conviction, the Supreme Court stated that, "We can not sanction this extended delay, resulting in confession, without subordinating the general rule of prompt arraignment to the discretion of arresting officers finding exceptional circumstances for its disregard." Here the Court did not consider the "free and voluntary" test but reversed the decision because there had been a delay in bringing the accused before the United States Commissioner.

---

[7] *Lego v. Twomey*, 404 U.S. 477, 30 L.Ed.2d 618, 92 S.Ct. 619 (1972).

[8] 318 U.S. 332, 87 L.Ed. 819, 63 S.Ct. 608 (1943).

[9] 354 U.S. 449, 1 L.Ed.2d 1479, 77 S.Ct. 1356 (1957).

The delay in arraignment (McNabb-Mallory) rule was at first applicable only in federal cases. Initially, the states refused to adopt the rule, but in 1961 the rule was made applicable in state courts as well.[10]

Because the *Mallory* case did not state nor define what was "unnecessary delay," hundreds of cases have been decided in an attempt to reach a definition. It is only "unnecessary" delays that make the statement inadmissible. If there is a necessary delay, for example a magistrate is not available, the confession will be admissible if otherwise qualified.[11]

If the arrest is made in the evening and the practice is not to bring the arrestee before the magistrate until the next morning, a confession will probably be admissible. On the other hand, if the arrest is made during the office hours of the judicial officer and there is no justification for not taking the person arrested before the judicial officer for a hearing, the delay will probably be considered as an unnecessary delay. Each case must be determined on the facts of that case. For example, the Indiana Court of Appeals for the First District found that a delay of twenty-six hours should not in itself render a confession, obtained during that period, inadmissible.[12]

To avoid problems, it is preferable to take the person arrested before a magistrate within a reasonable time. If the usual practice is followed and the person arrested is not discriminated against, the confession will probably be admissible. On the other hand, if the usual practice is to take an arrestee before a magistrate the morning following the arrest made the previous evening, and the suspect is not taken before the magistrate as is the customary procedure, a confession obtained during the delay will probably not be admissible.

§7.4   Warning and waiver requirements (Miranda rule)

In 1966 the Supreme Court of the United States added a third legal hurdle. In the now well known and well dramatized *Miranda* case, the majority concluded that when an individual is taken into custody or otherwise deprived of his freedom by the authorities and is subject to questioning, he must be given the follow warnings:

---

[10] *Culombe v. Connecticut*, 367 U.S. 568, 6 L.Ed.2d 1037, 81 S.Ct. 1860 (1961).

[11] *United States v. Mitchell*, 322 U.S. 65, 88 L.Ed. 1140, 64 S.Ct. 896 (1944).

[12] *Apple v. State*, __Ind. App.__, 304 N.E.2d 321 (1974). Also see the legislation which provides for a six-hour delay in federal cases, Omnibus Crime Control and Safe Streets Act of 1968, 701(c), 82 Stat. 210, 18 U.S.C. § 3501(c) (1970).

1. You have the right to remain silent and say nothing.
2. If you make a statement anything you say can and will be used against you in a court of law.
3. You have the right to have an attorney present.
4. If you cannot afford an attorney, one will be appointed for you prior to any questioning if you so desire.[13]

Not only must these warnings be given initially, but opportunity to exercise these rights must be afforded throughout the questioning. If the accused indicates at any stage of the questioning that he does not wish to be interrogated or that he wishes to consult with an attorney, the questioning must stop.

As is the case with other constitutional rights, this right may be voluntarily, knowingly, and intelligently waived. A waiver will not be presumed simply from the silence of the accused after the warnings are given. Also, the waiver will not be considered as voluntary if there is valid evidence that the accused was threatened, tricked, or cajoled.

The warnings are not required unless the individual is "taken into custody" and is "subject to questioning."

a. Judicial interpretation of "custody"

In the *Miranda* case, the Supreme Court indicated that the warnings must be administered if the accused is "in custody or otherwise deprived of his freedom of action in any significant way." Both the Supreme Court and lower courts have been called upon to determine the meaning of these words. In one Circuit Court of Appeals, the majority of the justices agreed that a suspect who was surrounded at his place of business by twenty armed agents was "in custody" as he was not free to leave and evidence obtained after he had been asked if he had any concealed weapons nearby was not admissible.[14] Another Circuit Court, however, found that the suspect was not in custody even when questioned at a police establishment because she had never attempted to leave and appeared at the police headquarters of her own free will.[15]

The United States Supreme Court, too, has been called upon to apply the rule to the specific facts of cases. In one of these cases, the Court reasoned that the suspect was in custody when officers entered his bedroom and ques-

---

[13] *Miranda v. Arizona*, 384 U.S. 436, 16 L.Ed.2d 1694, 86 S.Ct. 1602 (1966).
[14] *United States v. Castellana*, 488 F.2d 65 (5th Cir. 1974).
[15] *Freije v. United States*, 408 F.2d 100 (1st Cir. 1969).

tioned him in the early hours of the morning. Here, the officers admitted upon questioning that the suspect was not free to leave.[16] But where a burglary suspect was invited to the police station and appeared of his own free will, he was not "in custody" under a more recent decision.[17] Some of the news media indicated that the *Mathiason* case in effect reversed the *Miranda* decision. This, of course, is not factual as the decision merely more specifically defined "custody." This paragraph from the case more fully explains the Court's thinking:

> In the present case, however, there is no indication that the questioning took place in the context where respondent's freedom to depart was restricted in any way. He came voluntarily to the police station, where he was immediately informed that he was not under arrest. At the close of one-half hour's interview, respondent did in fact leave the police station without hindrance. It is clear from these facts that *Mathiason* was not in custody "or otherwise deprived of his freedom of action in any significant way."

The facts to be considered when the court is requested to determine if the person interviewed is in custody are: (1) the number of officers present, (2) the attitude toward the person being questioned, (3) the stage of the investigation, whether the investigation is still in the investigatory stage, (4) the environment where the interview takes place, and (5) if the interviewee is free to leave. It should be noted, however, that the determining factor is not whether the suspect is in his home or in the police station, but whether he is, in fact, free to leave.

As a practical matter, the suspect may not be in custody during the initial stages of the interview, but at some time during the interview facts may be developed which indicate knowledge of the crime, in which case the suspect would not be free to leave. If the officer has made such a determination or if the court finds that such a determination should logically have been made under the circumstances, the suspect is then in custody and the *Miranda* warnings must be administered if questioning continues.

An issue which is of considerable concern to police officers, especially those involved in traffic, is whether a person who is stopped for a traffic misdemeanor offense is in custody so as to require the *Miranda* warnings. The United States Supreme Court was asked to make this determination in the case of *Berkemer v. McCarty*.[18]

---

[16] *Orozco v. Texas*, 394 U.S. 324, 22 L.Ed.2d 311, 89 S.Ct. 1095 (1969).

[17] *Oregon v. Mathiason*, 429 U.S. 711, 50 L.Ed.2d 714, 97 S.Ct. 711 (1977).

[18] *Berkemer v. McCarty*, 468 U.S. 420, 82 L.Ed.2d 31, 104 S.Ct. 3138 (1984).

In the *Berkemer* case, the Sixth Circuit Court had ruled that a person stopped for a misdemeanor traffic offense could not be questioned until given the *Miranda* warnings. The United States Supreme Court by an eight-to-one majority decided that roadside questioning during a routine traffic stop does not constitute custodial interrogation unless the officer subjects the motorist to treatment that renders him in custody for practical purposes. The majority reasoned that the concerns underpinning *Miranda* are absent in a routine minor traffic stop situation. The Court continued by explaining that the traffic stop is usually temporary, brief and public, and that the relatively non-coercive nature of routine traffic stops makes this more analogous to investigative stops than arrests.

If, however, the treatment of the violator is such that it, in fact, renders him "in custody" for practical purposes, he will be entitled to the full protection prescribed by *Miranda*.

The rule then succinctly stated is that roadside questioning of a motorist detained pursuant to a routine traffic stop does not constitute custodial interrogation for *Miranda* purposes, but as soon as freedom of action is curtailed to a degree associated with a formal arrest, the *Miranda* warnings must be administered if questioning continues.

b.   Judicial determination of "questioning"

The Court in the *Miranda* case indicated that when an individual is taken into custody *and subjected to questioning*, the privilege against self-incrimination is jeopardized. If no questions are asked even though the suspect is in custody, the *Miranda* warnings are not required. If, for example, the suspect is taken into custody and, without questioning, voluntarily admits his guilt on the way to the station, the statements will be admissible. Also, a general inquiry at the scene of the crime will not be considered questioning so as to make the volunteered statements inadmissible. Following this reasoning, a majority of the members of the Illinois Appellate Court refused to exclude statements given to the officers when they arrived at the scene of a crime and asked, "What happened?". Such statements are admissible as responses to general on-the-scene questioning by the police as to facts surrounding the crime.[19]

"What is 'questioning'?" While it would seem that questioning is asking questions, this is not necessarily the definition promulgated by the courts. Questioning not only includes asking direct questions to the suspect, but

---

[19]   *People v. Routt*, 100 Ill.App.2d 388, 241 N.E.2d 206 (1968).

words or actions on the part of the officer which would reasonably be likely to elicit incriminating responses from the suspect.[20]

In the *Innis* case, the suspect and two of the arresting officers were in the car when the officers, without bringing the suspect into the conversation, engaged in a conversation between themselves concerning a missing shotgun. One of the officers stated that there were "a lot of handicapped children running around in this area and God forbid one of them might find a weapon with shells and they might hurt themselves." The statement was not directed to the suspect nor did the officers indicate they expected an answer. However, the suspect interrupted the conversation, suggesting that the officers should turn the car around so he could show them where the gun was located.

After the State Supreme Court set aside the conviction, the United States Supreme Court stated the rule as to what is "questioning" or "interrogation."

> We conclude that *Miranda* safeguards come into play whenever a person in custody is subjected to either express questioning or its functional equivalent. That is to say, the term "interrogation" under *Miranda* refers not only to express questioning, but also to any words or actions on the part of the police...that the police should know are reasonably likely to elicit incriminating responses from the suspect.

In the *Innis* case, after stating the rule, the court found that the dialogue between the two officers did not amount to "interrogation." Nevertheless, the rule has been clearly defined and must be applied in future cases.

In a more recent case, the Supreme Court again was confronted with the question as to whether the activities of the officers involved amounted to questioning after the suspect had indicated his intention not to answer any questions.[21] At the insistence of the defendant's wife, she was allowed to meet with the defendant in the office where the defendant had been interviewed. The police agreed to the meeting on the condition that an officer be present and that the conversation be recorded. During the meeting in which the wife expressed despair, the defendant told her not to answer any questions until a lawyer was present. The prosecution used the information on the tape to rebut the defendant's insanity defense, and the defendant was convicted and sentenced to death.

The Supreme Court ruled that this activity was not "questioning," as the police officers did not directly question, nor did they use subterfuge or a

---

[20] *Rhode Island v. Innis*, 446 U.S. 289, 64 L.Ed.2d 297, 100 S.Ct. 1682 (1980).
[21] *Colorado v. Connelley*, __ U.S.__, 93 L.Ed.2d 473, 107 S.Ct. 515 (1986).

"psychological ploy" to try to get the suspect to say something incriminating. In rejecting the claim that this was questioning, the Court explained: "Officers do not interrogate a suspect simply by hoping he will incriminate himself."

The rule gleaned from these cases is that "questioning" includes express questioning or its fundamental equivalent, that is, any words or actions on the part of the police that the police should know are reasonably likely to elicit an incriminating response from the suspect. However, merely allowing the suspect to make statements is not questioning.

c.   Interpretation of "warning" and "waiver"

If the suspect has been taken into custody and questions are anticipated, a warning is required. The suspect may waive his rights, but he must do so knowingly and voluntarily. The prosecution must demonstrate that the warnings were given and the protected rights were waived by the suspect. A waiver will not be presumed simply from the silence of the accused after the warnings are given, nor will a waiver be considered as voluntary if there is valid evidence that the accused was threatened into giving the waiver. Not only must the warnings be given initially, but opportunity to exercise these rights must be afforded throughout the questioning.

The *Miranda* case provided that a suspect must be warned when he is in custody and prior to questioning. If there is both custody and questioning, then the warnings stated in *Miranda* are appropriate. The question which arose in the case of *California v. Prysock* was whether the warnings must be given in the exact terms as stated in the *Miranda* case.[22]

In the *Prysock* case, a murder suspect was given the warnings, but not in the exact terms as stated in the *Miranda* case. The Court of Appeals reversed the conviction and ordered a new trial because the *Miranda* warnings were not given in the exact terms. The lower court had ruled that the defendant had not been properly advised of his right to the services of an attorney before and during the interrogation. The United States Supreme Court disagreed in holding that "nothing in these observations suggests any desirable rigidity in the form of the required warnings."

While the *Miranda* warnings need not be given in the exact terms as they are printed in the *Miranda* case, any substitute must meet the "fully effective equivalent test." It is preferable to give the *Miranda* warnings in the form that they appear in the case. However, if the warnings effectively advise the suspect of his rights, the confession will most likely be admitted.

---

[22] *California v. Prysock*, 453 U.S. 355, 69 L.Ed.2d 696, 101 S.Ct. 2806 (1981).

Allowing some flexibility, the Supreme Court has also indicated that there is no legal requirement that the suspect make an express statement that he waives his rights after the *Miranda* warnings have been given.[23] In the *Butler* case, the lower reviewing court reversed a conviction because the suspect had said during the interview that "I will talk with you but I am not signing any form." The lower court indicated that this was not a specific waiver as required by *Miranda*. The United States Supreme Court disagreed, advising that the *Miranda* case did not hold that an express statement is indispensable to a finding of a waiver. The question of waiver is not one of form but of substance. The prosecution must demonstrate that the defendant knowingly and voluntarily waived his rights, but the waiver may be in the form of actions of indirect affirmation.

If the suspect indicates during the questioning or prior to the questioning that he does not want to answer questions or he has invoked his right to counsel, the questioning must cease. In 1981 the United States Supreme Court formulated the rule which has become known as the "*Edwards Rule*".[24]

In the *Edwards* case, after the police had advised the suspect of his rights, he answered, "I want an attorney before making a deal." Questioning ceased at that time, but two detectives, who were colleagues of the officers who interrogated Edwards the previous night, came to the jail to see Edwards. After being told by a guard that he had to talk to the two officers, the officers again informed the suspect of his *Miranda* rights, and Edwards indicated that he was willing to talk, but he first wanted to hear the taped statements of an alleged accomplice. He thereafter implicated himself in the crime and was convicted. The Arizona Supreme Court held that he waived his right to remain silent and his right to counsel when he voluntarily gave the statement after being informed of his rights the second time. The United States Supreme Court, however, disagreed with these comments:

> We further hold that an accused, such as Edwards, having expressed his desire to deal with police only through counsel, is not subject to further investigation by the authorities until counsel has been made available to him, *unless the accused himself initiates further communications, exchanges, or conversations* with the police. (Emphasis added)

---

[23] *North Carolina v. Butler*, 441 U.S. 369, 60 L.Ed.2d 286, 99 S.Ct. 1755 (1979).

[24] *Edwards v. Arizona*, 451 U.S. 477, 68 L.Ed.2d 378, 101 S.Ct. 1880 (1981). This rule was reaffirmed in 1984 in the Case of *Solem v. Stumes*, 465 U.S. 638, 79 L.Ed.2d 579, 104 S.Ct. 1338 (1984).

But once an accused "knowingly and intelligently" elects to proceed without counsel, the uncounseled statements he then makes need not be excluded at trial.[25] *Miranda* warnings are sufficient to make the accused aware of his counsel rights.

Several cases have interpreted the Edwards Rule. In one case, the Supreme Court determined that a suspect who claimed his right to counsel "initiated further questioning" when he asked the officers, "Well, what is going to happen to me now?"[26]

In a more recent case, the Supreme Court was again asked to determine if the "Edwards Rule" applies when a defendant has requested counsel, questioning has ceased, but the interrogation concerning an unrelated crime is initiated by enforcement agents.[27] In the *Roberson* case, the suspect, after being arrested at the scene of a burglary and advised of his *Miranda* rights, replied that he wanted a lawyer before answering his questions. Questioning ceased at this point, but three days later, while the suspect was still in custody, a different officer, unaware that the suspect had earlier requested counsel, advised him of his rights and interrogated him about a different burglary, obtaining an incriminating statement concerning that crime. At the trial, this statement was suppressed in reliance upon the decision in the *Edwards* case, and the Arizona Court of Appeals affirmed the suppression.

The United States Supreme Court agreed with the Arizona Court of Appeals that the Edwards Rule applies even though the suspect was reinterrogated by a different officer about an unrelated offense. In concluding their opinion, the majority commented:

> Whether a contemplated reinterrogation concerns the same or a different offense, or whether the same or different law enforcement authorities are involved in the second investigation, the same need to determine whether the suspect has requested counsel exists. The police department's failure to honor that request cannot be justified by the lack of diligence of a particular officer.

In another case, the majority of the Supreme Court agreed that the suspect had waived his right to counsel when he told the officers he was willing to *talk* about the incident but that he would not make a written statement.[28] Here, the suspect was advised three times by the police of his right to counsel

---

[25] *Patterson v. Illinois*, 56 LW 4733 decided June 24, 1988.

[26] *Oregon v. Bradshaw*, 462 U.S. 1039, 77 L.Ed.2d 405, 103 S.Ct. 2830 (1983).

[27] *Arizona v. Roberson*, __ U.S. __, __ L.Ed.2d __, 108 S.Ct. 2093 (1988).

[28] *Connecticut v. Barrett*, __ U.S. __, 93 L.Ed.2d 920, 107 S.Ct. 828 (1987).

and each time agreed to make an oral statement. Succinctly stating the reason for allowing the statement to be admitted, the Court made this comment:

> The fact that officials took the opportunity provided by Barret to obtain an oral confession is quite consistent with the Fifth Amendment. *Miranda* gives the defendant the right to choose between speech and silence, and Barret chose to speak.

Do statements by the defendant without the *Miranda* warnings necessarily contaminate later statements made after the warnings have been given? This issue reached the highest court after the defendant was convicted of burglary and appealed.[29]

In *Oregon v. Elstad*, the suspect, without having the warnings given, was asked some preliminary questions at his home concerning the burglary and replied, "Yes, I was there," thereby implicating himself. After he had been transported to the Sheriff's Headquarters approximately one hour later, he was advised for the first time of his *Miranda* rights. At this point, the defendant waived his right to counsel as well as his rights under the Fifth Amendment and agreed to make a statement.

The Oregon Court of Appeals reversed the conviction, noting that the "cat was sufficiently out of the bag" when the first questions were asked and this had a coercive impact on the later admission. The United States Supreme Court, however, distinguished this from the *Edwards* situation, as here no *Miranda* warnings had been given and counsel had not been requested. That Court made this comment:

> It is an unwarranted extension of *Miranda* to hold that a simple failure to administer the warnings unaccompanied by any actual coercion or circumstances calculated to undermine the suspect's ability to exercise his free will, so taints the investigatory process that a subsequent, voluntary and informed waiver is ineffective.

If coercion or improper tactics are used in obtaining an unwarned statement, then the *Elstad* ruling would not apply; that is, such improper tactics in obtaining the first statement would so contaminate the second statement that it would be inadmissible even if the warnings were administered before the second statement. Also, if the suspect has requested counsel, with or without warnings, the questioning must cease unless the suspect himself initiates further questioning.

---

[29] *Oregon v. Elstad*, 470 U.S. 298, 84 L.Ed.2d 222, 105 S.Ct. 1285 (1985).

§7.5   Exclusion of confession as a means of enforcing the Fourth Amendment

In addition to those challenges discussed in the preceding sections, statements introduced in court may be challenged on a fourth ground. This challenge relies on the "fruit of the poisonous tree" doctrine, sometimes referred to as the "Wong Sun" doctrine. Simply stated, this rule provides that if the confession is derived immediately from an unlawful arrest or unlawful search, the confession is "tainted" and neither it nor its fruits may be used against the defendant whose Fourth Amendment rights are violated.

In the case of *Wong Sun v. United States*, an oral statement implicating one of the accused was held inadmissible because it was made immediately following an unlawful entry and an unlawful arrest.[30] After finding that the arrest was illegal, the judge reasoned that such statements were fruits of the agent's unlawful action and that the exclusionary prohibition relating to evidence obtained by illegal search extends to the indirect as well as to the direct products of such invasions.

Even if the suspect who is arrested illegally is given the *Miranda* warnings, there is a good possibility that the confession obtained after these warnings will remain contaminated. In a case which was before the Supreme Court in 1975, a confession was obtained after a clearly investigatory arrest. Prior to the questioning, the officers properly advised the arrestee of his rights, and the accused voluntarily agreed to make statements to the police. The prosecution argued that as the defendant had waived his Fifth Amendment rights voluntarily, the fact that here was an illegal arrest preceding the advice should not taint his confession.[31]

Mr. Justice Blackmun, speaking for the majority, noted that there was a causal connection between the illegality of the arrest and the confession, and that giving the *Miranda* warnings alone does not attenuate the taint of the illegal arrest. The majority of the Court agreed in effect that the Fifth Amendment rights are protected by giving the *Miranda* warnings but that this in itself does not protect the Fourth Amendment rights; despite *Miranda* warnings, the Fourth and Fourteenth Amendments require the exclusion from evidence of statements obtained as a fruit of an arrest which the arresting officer knows, or should have known, was without probable cause and therefore unconstitutional.

Three cases have reaffirmed the rule that a confession is contaminated if there is a causal connection between the confession and an illegal search or

---

[30]   371 U.S. 471, 9 L.Ed.2d 441, 83 S.Ct. 407 (1963).
[31]   *Brown v. Illinois*, 422 U.S. 590, 45 L.Ed.2d 416, 95 S.Ct. 2254 (1975).

arrest. In the case of *Dunaway v. New York*, the Supreme Court reversed the conviction of a suspect where incriminating statements and sketches were obtained during the petitioner's illegal detention. There the Court pointed out that:

> Where there is a close causal connection between the illegal search and the confession, not only is the exclusion of the evidence more likely to deter similar conduct in the future, but the use of the evidence is more likely to compromise the integrity of the courts.[32]

In a second case, in 1982 the Supreme Court ruled that a robbery suspect's confession, six hours after his illegal arrest, was not sufficiently purged of the taint of that illegality to render it admissible in evidence.[33]

In a third case, the Court reiterated the rule that a confession which follows immediately after an illegal arrest or search will not be admissible if there is a causal connection between the illegality of the arrest and the statement, even though the *Miranda* warnings have been given. Emphasizing this point, the Supreme Court made this comment:

> Under well-established precedent, the fact that a confession may be voluntary for purposes of the Fifth Amendment, in the sense that the *Miranda* warnings were given and understood, is not by itself sufficient to purge the taint of the illegal arrest.[34]

From these cases, a clear rule evolves. A confession obtained by exploitation of an illegal arrest and/or search will not be admitted if challenged by the defendant.

§7.6   Right to counsel

Failure of the officer to permit a person who is asked incriminating questions to consult with counsel will invalidate the confession. This rule was established in the now well known case of *Escobedo v. Illinois*.[35] In the *Escobedo* case, the defendant was arrested for the first time and released on the same day on a writ of habeas corpus. He told the police nothing at the time. He was rearrested about eleven days later and, before making any statement,

---

[32] *Dunaway v. New York*, 442 U.S. 200, 60 L.Ed.2d 824, 99 S.Ct. 2248 (1979).

[33] *Taylor v. Alabama*, 457 U.S. 687, 73 L.Ed.2d 314, 102 S.Ct. 2664 (1982).

[34] *Lanier v. South Carolina*, 474 U.S. 25, 88 L.Ed.2d 23, 106 S.Ct. 297 (1985).

[35] 378 U.S. 478, 12 L.Ed.2d 977, 84 S.Ct. 1758 (1964).

requested an opportunity to consult with his attorney. His attorney likewise made repeated efforts to gain access to his client. Each man was told that he could not see the other until the police had finished with the interrogation. In the course of questioning, the defendant stated that another person had committed the shooting, thereby admitting knowledge of the crime and implicating himself. At the trial, he moved to suppress the incriminating statements, but his motion was denied.

The United States Supreme Court in reversing the conviction and declaring the confession inadmissible designated the precise point in the criminal process when the right to counsel attaches. The Court's decision concluded with the admonition that:

> When the process shifts from the investigatory to the accusatory-- when its focus is on the accused and its purpose is to elicit a confession--our adversary system begins to operate, and, under the circumstances here, the accused must be permitted to consult with his lawyer.

In the *Escobedo* case, the accused actually requested to consult with his lawyer. Following that case, the question was asked, "what if the defendant had been ignorant of his rights and had not made a demand on the police?" "Must he be advised in every case of his right to counsel?" These questions were apparently answered in the *Miranda* case discussed earlier, where the Supreme Court made the sweeping mandate that the prosecution may not use statements stemming from custodial interrogation of the defendant unless, prior to questioning, the person has been warned that he has a right to the presence of an attorney, either retained or appointed by the court. The Court continued by stating, "If he indicates in any manner and at any stage of the process that he wishes to consult with an attorney before speaking there can be no further questioning.[36]

In the *Miranda* case, the majority decided that a suspect who is in custody must be advised of his right to counsel prior to questioning. Also, a suspect who is in custody must be allowed to consult with an attorney, if he so requests, prior to any questioning. But is it necessary for the police to advise the suspect in custody that an attorney has been retained by someone else to represent him? The Supreme Court in the case of *Moran v. Burbine* answered this in the negative.[37]

In the *Moran* case, the suspect was arrested on a breaking and entering charge. Unknown to the defendant, his sister, who was unaware that the sus-

---

[36] *Escobedo v. Illinois, supra* n. 23.

[37] *Moran v. Burbine,* __U.S.__, 89 L.Ed.2d 410, 106 S.Ct. 1135 (1986).

pect was under suspicion of another charge, sought help from the public defender's office. The assistant public defender agreed to represent the suspect and telephoned the detective division stating that she would act as the defendant's counsel. She was informed that the suspect would not be questioned until the next day.

The defendant was not advised that counsel had been retained to represent him nor that counsel had contacted the detective. He did, however, validly waive his self-incrimination and counsel rights after being warned and made a confession. In a habeas corpus proceeding, the defendant argued that the police conduct, in failing to inform him about the attorney's call and in conducting interviews after telling the attorney there would be no interviews, tainted his waivers. The Federal Court of Appeals agreed, and the case went to the United States Supreme Court.

The majority of the Court determined that the confession should be admitted, expressing this reasoning:

> The police failure to inform the respondent of the attorney's telephone call did not deprive him of information essential to his ability to knowingly waive his right to remain silent and to the presence of counsel.

The reasoning is that as the suspect himself was aware of his right to counsel and Fifth Amendment rights; the fact that he was not advised that counsel had been retained and the fact that counsel had not been advised concerning the questioning did not influence his ability to make his decision.

Had the suspect requested counsel or had he been denied permission to contact counsel before making the statements, the decision in the *Moran* case would have been different.

The right to counsel protection comes into play also where an informant cellmate obtains information from an indicated defendant at the request of law enforcement officials. As the rule in the cellmate cases is very technical, it is necessary to discuss two cases with different results.

In the first of these cases, the informant who was the cellmate of the defendant was advised by an FBI agent to be alert to any statements made, but not to initiate any communications with or question the defendant.[38] After the informant had initiated a discussion, the defendant did, in fact, tell the informant some details of the crime, and the informant testified at the trial. The United States Supreme Court reversed the conviction, including this statement in its decision:

---

[38] *United States v. Henry*, 447 U.S. 264, 65 L.Ed.2d 115, 100 S.Ct. 2183 (1980).

> By intentionally creating a situation likely to induce Henry to make
> incriminating statements without the assistance of counsel, the gov-
> ernment violated Henry's Sixth Amendment right to counsel.

In the *Henry* case, the cellmate informant had not asked questions directly
but had stimulated the conversation. In a more recent case, the informant
obeyed the police instructions to only listen to the defendant for the purposes
of identifying his confederates in the robbery and murder, but not to question
about any crimes.[39] The majority of the Supreme Court distinguished this
case from the *Henry* case, noting that the Sixth Amendment does not forbid
admission of an accused's statement made to a jailhouse informant who is
placed in close proximity to the defendant in the jail, but who makes no effort
to stimulate the conversation about the crime with which the defendant is
charged. If the informant cellmate merely listens and does not elicit any incriminating remarks, the right to counsel is not violated even if the suspect
has been indicted and counsel appointed.

In an interesting comment in the *Kullman* case, the Supreme Court indicated that the burden is on the defendant to demonstrate that the police and
their informant took some action, beyond merely listening, that was designed
deliberately to elicit incriminating remarks. If the defendant does not prove
improper action on the part of the police or informant, the statements made
to the informant are admissible.

As in the case of the waiver of Fifth Amendment rights, the accused may
waive his Sixth Amendment right to counsel if he does so voluntarily, knowingly, and intelligently. According to the Eighth Circuit Court of Appeals,
there is "no compelling reason to hold that he (the accused) may not voluntarily, knowingly, and intelligently waive his right to have counsel present at
an interrogation after counsel has been appointed."[40] But the burden is always upon the government to show that the waiver was knowingly and intelligently made.

§7.7   Corroboration

A fundamental rule of law has developed in this country. This rule is that
a confession standing alone will not support a conviction. The state must introduce evidence independent of the confession to show that a crime has
been committed. It is sufficient if the outside proof together with the confes-

---

[39] *Kullman v. Wilson*, __U.S.__, 91 L.Ed.2d 364, 106 S.Ct. 2616 (1986).
[40] *Moore v. Wolff*, 495 F.2d 35 (8th Cir. 1974).

sion satisfies the jury beyond a reasonable doubt that a crime has, in fact, been committed. Some states have by statute codified this requirement and state in such statutes that the *corpus delicti* be proved by independent proof.

The rule that a confession must be corroborated was developed because some suspects were found guilty and even put to death when there had been no crime. Under the early English laws, confessions had been admissible even if there was no independent evidence to prove the guilt of the accused. Recognizing the possibility of irreparable mistakes, the corroboration rule was recognized from the very beginning in this country.

§7.8   Derivative evidence

Neither real evidence derived as a result of an involuntary confession nor the confession itself may be used to prove the guilt of the defendant. To state this differently, the "fruit of the poisonous tree" doctrine unquestionably applies to real evidence obtained by means of an invalid confession. After discussing the warnings which must be given prior to questioning, the Court in the *Miranda* case declared:

> But unless and until such warnings and waiver are demonstrated by the prosecution at trial, no evidence obtained as a result of the interrogation can be used against him.

But this rule does not apply to testimony given by a witness discovered as a result of questioning. If the failure to advise a suspect of his rights to appointed counsel has no bearing on the reliability of a witness, the testimony of the discovered witness should not be excluded.[41] The fact that not only the confession or statement itself but tangible evidence derived therefrom will be inadmissible if proper safeguards are not followed makes it even more essential that all who are involved in the criminal justice process are thoroughly conversant with the rules relating to admissions and confessions.

§7.9   Admissible statements (including "good faith" exception)

Too often the police investigator, after reading Supreme Court decisions, is convinced that no questioning is authorized and no statements will be admissible. This is not the case. The Supreme Court in the *Miranda* decision

---

[41] *Michigan v. Tucker*, 417 U.S. 433, 41 L.Ed.2d 182, 94 S.Ct. 2357 (1974).

emphasized that the Court did not purport to find all confessions inadmissible. The Court remarked, "Confessions remain a proper element in law enforcement." The Court went on to explain that statements given freely and voluntarily are admissible. The justices also reminded the reader that the police are not required to stop a person who enters the station and states that he wishes to confess to a crime, or a person who calls the police to make a confession or make any other statement.

In addition, the courts in recent years have established specific instances where confessions may be admissible even though some of the technical rules have not been followed. Some of these are discussed in the following paragraphs.

a.   Use of statements for impeachment purposes

Even if a confession is inadmissible to establish the prosecutor's "case in chief" because the *Miranda* warnings were not administered, that confession may nevertheless be admissible to impeach the credibility of the defendant if he takes the stand in his own behalf.[42]   Chief Justice Burger speaking for the majority of the Supreme Court explained the reasoning of the majority in approving the use of confession for limited impeachment purposes:

> Every criminal defendant is privileged to testify in his own defense or to refuse to do so. But that privilege cannot be construed to include the right to commit perjury...having voluntarily taken the stand, petitioner was under an obligation to speak truthfully and accurately, and the prosecution here did no more than utilize the traditional truth-testing devices in the adversary process.

The majority of the Supreme Court in 1975 reiterated its approval of the limited use of custodial statements for impeachment purposes.[43]

While custodial statements inadmissible under *Miranda* may nonetheless be admissible for limited impeachment purposes, silence of the accused after warnings may not be used for impeachment purposes.[44]   As an accused has the right to remain silent during police interrogation, any reference to his silence under such circumstances carries with it an intolerable prejudicial impact. The police therefore are not justified in relying on the "tactic confession" in proving guilt of the suspect or even for impeachment purposes.

---

[42]   *Harris v. New York*, 401 U.S. 222, 28 L.Ed.2d 1, 91 S.Ct. 643 (1971).

[43]   *Oregon v. Hass*, 420 U.S. 714, 43 L.Ed.2d 570, 95 S.Ct. 1215 (1975).

[44]   *United States v. Hale*, 422 U.S. 171, 45 L.Ed.2d 99, 95 S.Ct. 2133 (1975).

b.   Use of statements made at the grand jury hearings

Chief Justice Burger, speaking for the majority of the Court, rendered the decision that the *Miranda* warnings need not be given a grand jury witness who is called upon to testify about criminal activities in which he may be personally involved.[45]   The Court in making this decision indicated that the warnings enumerated in the *Miranda* case were aimed at the evil seen by the Court as endemic to police interrogation of a person in custody.   These warnings need not be necessarily required in other situations, the Court concluded.

c.   Non-official questioning

In the absence of state involvement, voluntary statements made to private citizens are admissible even if no *Miranda* warnings are given.   As in the case of the Fourth Amendment, the Fifth Amendment prohibitions operate only against official action.   Therefore, if a private individual obtains information without the encouragement or knowledge of the police officer, that evidence is admissible even if no warnings are given.

Nonetheless, as the free and voluntary rule is based in part on the rule of evidence (the evidence must be trustworthy), the defendant would have grounds for challenge if force were used, even if this force were exerted by a private citizen.   On the other hand, if the challenge is predicated only on the *Miranda* rule or the delay in arraignment rule, the statements made to a private person would no doubt be admissible.[46]

d.   Public Safety Exception

After twenty years of adherence to the literal language of the *Miranda* decision, which provided that evidence would not be admissible unless the warnings were given, the Supreme Court acknowledged in 1984 that it was time to pull back.   Speaking through Justice Rehnquist, the majority announced a narrow "public safety exception" to the requirement that a suspect be advised of his rights prior to custodial interrogation.[47]

---

[45]   *United States v. Mandujano*, 425 U.S. 564, 48 L.Ed.2d 212, 96 S.Ct. 1768 (1976).

[46]   *United States v. Casteel*, 476 F.(2d) 152 (10th Cir. 1973); *Commonwealth v. Mahnke*, __Mass.__, 335 N.E.2d 660 (1975), *cert. denied*, 425 U.S. 959 (1976).

[47]   *New York v. Quarles*, 467 U.S. 649, 81 L.Ed.2d 550, 104 S.Ct. 2626 (1984).

In the *Quarles* case, a police officer entered a grocery store after being told by a rape victim that her assailant had entered the supermarket and warned that the assailant was carrying a gun. After the suspect was apprehended in the grocery store, the officer noticed that the suspect was wearing an empty shoulder holster. At this point, the officer asked the suspect, "Where is the gun?" The suspect indicated that the gun was in some empty cartons and said, "The gun is over there." The suspect was in custody-- questions were asked--the *Miranda* warnings were not administered.

The trial court concluded that the statement "The gun is over there" was not admissible because it was tainted by the *Miranda* violation. This decision was upheld by both the Supreme Court of New York and the New York Court of Appeals.

The United States Supreme Court, in overruling the state courts, coined what has become known as the "public safety exception" to the *Miranda* requirement. The majority indicated that the need for answers in this situation outweighs the need for a prophylactic rule.

Succinctly stated, the rule in the *Quarles* case is that when police officers ask questions reasonably prompted by a concern for public safety, the suspect's incriminating statements may be admitted into evidence even if the *Miranda* warnings are not administered.

In applying this rule, the officer must be aware that this is a very narrow exception to the rule that the *Miranda* warnings must be given when the suspect is in custody and prior to the questioning.

§7.10   Admissibility of a second confession after an inadmissible first confession

If a confession is obtained in violation of the Constitution as interpreted by the courts, that confession and derivative evidence will not be admitted, with some exceptions as discussed. The question that arises is whether an inadmissible first confession will taint a second confession. As a general rule, once a confession has been made under improper influences, the presumption arises that a subsequent confession of the same crime flows from the same influences even though made to a different person than the one to whom the first confession was made.[48] If, however, the police ask preliminary questions without giving the *Miranda* warnings and later continue the questioning after the full *Miranda* warnings have been administered, state-

---

[48] *Payne v. State*, 231 Ark. 727, 332 S.W.2d 233, (1960). *Westover v. United States*, 384 U.S. 436, 16 L.Ed.2d 694, 86 S.Ct. 1602 (1966). Note: Part of the *Miranda v. Arizona* decision.

ments made at the first session do not necessarily contaminate those made at the second session.[49]

In the *Elstad* case, the Court conceded that if there was no deliberate coercion or improper tactics in obtaining the first unwarned statement a careful and thorough administration of the *Miranda* warnings before a secured interview would cure the condition that rendered the unwarned statement inadmissible.

Obviously, if coercion tactics are used in obtaining the first confession or first statement, then the second statement would be inadmissible even if the *Miranda* warnings were given in full at the time the second statement is taken.

§7.11 Summary

Although the courts have condemned improper questioning and have criticized the police for interrogating suspects rather than conducting thorough investigations, those same courts have specifically approved the use of questioning as a means of investigation when it is done within the established rules. To protect those who are accused of crime, many admissibility tests have been expounded and explained in this chapter.

The first and traditional test is the free and voluntary test. This provides that in order for a statement to be admissible into court, the prosecution has the burden of proving that the statement was made freely and voluntarily, i.e., without force or duress. Even if the confession is free and voluntary, it may not be admissible if the officer unnecessarily delays in taking the apprehended person before a judicial officer as required by law.

Perhaps the best known requirements are those established in the *Miranda* case in 1966. Here, the Supreme Court Justices established the rule that a confession will not be admissible unless the provisions established in that case were followed. In short, the *Miranda* rule provides that if a person is in custody and subject to questioning, he must be warned prior to any questioning that (1) he has a right to remain silent, (2) anything he says can and will be used against him in a court of law, (3) he has the right to the presence of an attorney, and (4) that if he cannot afford an attorney, one will be appointed for him prior to any questioning if he so desires. In addition to the warnings, the suspect must be provided an opportunity to exercise these rights throughout the questioning. If, however, he is not in custody or even if he is in custody and is not subject to questioning, the warnings are not neces-

---

[49] *Oregon v. Elstad*, 470 U.S. 298, 84 L.Ed.2d 222, 105 S.Ct. 1285 (1985).

sary. Also, these constitutional rights may be waived provided this waiver is made voluntarily, knowingly, and intelligently.

One method of enforcing the Sixth Amendment's right to counsel is to exclude a statement made by the defendant if this safeguard is not met. The accused, if in custody, must be warned of his right to counsel prior to questioning and must be afforded the opportunity to have counsel. Even if not in custody, the accused must be *permitted* to have counsel if incriminating questions are asked.

A confession that is free and voluntary, is not obtained during an unnecessary delay in arraignment, and is obtained after the suspect is given the *Miranda* warnings and waives his rights may nevertheless be inadmissible if it is derived immediately from an unlawful arrest and/or search. The reasoning is that a confession which derives immediately from an unlawful entry or an unlawful search is considered to be the fruit of an official illegality and therefore constitutionally tainted.

Finally, an extrajudicial confession standing alone will not support a conviction. Independent evidence must be introduced to corroborate the statements made in the confession.

Notwithstanding the requirements which must be met prior to the introduction of a confession in evidence, some statements are admissible. In the *Miranda* case, the Court specifically verified that confessions are admissible if they are free and voluntary. That Court also approved general on-the-scene questioning as to facts surrounding the crime. Later cases have indicated that the officer does not have to give the warnings as required in *Miranda* unless the suspect is in custody and is being questioned. A suspect will not be considered in custody if he is free to leave.

The Supreme Court has approved the use of the extrajudicial confession to impeach the in-court testimony of the defendant who takes the stand in his own behalf even though the *Miranda* warnings are not given. More recently, the Supreme Court has approved the rule that warnings need not be given to a grand jury witness who is called upon to testify about criminal activities, and statements made to private citizens without official involvement are admitted into evidence as only official conduct is prohibited by the Fifth Amendment.

The Supreme Court has relaxed the rules relating to the admission of a *Miranda*less confession and have reasoned that the *Miranda* warnings need not be administered prior to questioning if the safety of the officer or others reasonably requires that the questions be asked immediately.

In many instances, it is not necessary to question the suspect in order to make a case. Despite court restrictions, interrogation is still a useful and legitimate means of investigating crime. The knowledgeable officer will not only be aware of the questioning requirements but will be able to select the best investigative tool.

Chapter 8

PRE-TRIAL
IDENTIFICATION PROCEDURES

...the confrontation compelled by the State between the accused and the victim or witnesses to a crime to elicit identification evidence is peculiarly riddled with innumerable dangers and variable factors which might seriously, even crucially, derogate from a fair trial...[I]n practice the issue of identity may (in the absence of other relevant evidence) for all practical purposes be determined there and then, before the trial.

United States v. Wade,
388 U.S. 218, 18 L.Ed.2d 1149,
87 S.Ct. 1926 (1967)

Section
8.1   General considerations
8.2   Fingerprinting and photographing suspects
8.3   Lineup – self-incrimination challenge
8.4   Lineup – right to counsel challenge
8.5   Lineup – due process challenge
8.6   Pre-trial photographic identification
8.7   Dental examination

8.8   Voice exemplars

8.9   Footprint comparisons and other body examinations

8.10   Summary

§8.1   General considerations

As part of the investigation process, it is often appropriate or even essential to identify the suspect. As a rule, the first step after arrest is to fingerprint and photograph the suspect. Often it is good investigative practice to have the suspect appear before a victim or a witness to determine if the investigation is proceeding along the proper lines. Sometimes the confrontation immediately follows the apprehension in order to eliminate suspects, and sometimes the confrontation is by means of a lineup which might take place some days later. The taking of fingerprints and photographs and the confrontation for identification have been challenged on at least three constitutional grounds--self-incrimination, right to counsel, and due process.

The law relating to fingerprinting and photographing has developed over a period of years and is presently well established. The case decisions regarding the lineup and other confrontations for identification are in the process of developing and thus are not quite so well established. Contrary to what is commonly claimed, it is not the lineup or confrontation itself that is challenged. It is the in-court identification which might be contaminated by improper confrontation procedures that is objectionable. The danger is that the witness who is called upon to identify the suspect in court may make that identification not from what occurred at the scene of the crime but what occurred at the later confrontation for identification.

These issues will be presented and discussed in the sections that follow.

§8.2   Fingerprinting and photographing suspects

Although fingerprinting and photographing suspects is now common practice, these procedures have not always gone unchallenged. The primary challenge is that subjecting a person to fingerprinting and photographing for identification purposes requires the suspect to incriminate himself in violation of the Fifth Amendment. One of the early Supreme Court decisions in which this matter was an issue was *Holt. v. United States*.[1] In that case the majority distinguished between compelling a person to give verbal evidence and requiring him to allow his prints to be taken.

---

[1]   218 U.S. 245, 54 L.Ed. 1021, 31 S.Ct. 2 (1910).

The line of demarcation was clearly established in the case of *Schmerber v. California* where the Court stated:

> We hold that the privilege (self-incrimination) protects an accused only from being compelled to testify against himself or otherwise provide the state with evidence of a testimonial or communicative nature.[2]

Regarding the taking of fingerprints, the Supreme Court in that case made this comment:

> It [the self-incrimination privilege] offers no protection against compulsion to submit to fingerprinting, photographing, or measurements, to write or speak for identification, to appear in court, to stand, to assume a stance, to walk, or to make a particular gesture.

Clearly, the taking of palm prints or fingerprints does not violate the self-incrimination protection of the Constitution if the person in lawful custody is required to submit to photographing and fingerprinting as a part of a routine identification process.[3]   Nor is there any violation of the Fourth Amendment if the person whose fingerprints are taken has been properly arrested. If, however, the sole purpose of the detention is to obtain fingerprints and the arrest is not justified, the Fourth Amendment search and seizure provisions are violated and this becomes an illegal search.[4] However, the authorization by a judicial officer to schedule a time for the fingerprinting of a suspect may be proper even though the suspect has not been formally arrested.[5]

§8.3   Lineup – self-incrimination challenge

Although the lineup or other confrontation has been challenged on other constitutional grounds, as will be discussed, defendants have had little success in challenging this procedure as a violation of the self-incrimination protec-

---

[2]   *Schmerber v. California*, 384 U.S. 757, 16 L.Ed.2d 908, 86 S.Ct. 1826 (1966). *United States v. Doe*, 465 U.S. 605, 79 L.Ed.2d 552, 104 S.Ct. 1237 (1984).

[3]   *Smith v. United States*, 324 F.2d 879 (D.C. Cir. 1963).

[4]   *Davis v. Mississippi*, 394 U.S. 721, 22 L.Ed.2d 676, 89 S.Ct. 1394 (1969).

[5]   For a discussion of this point, see *Davis v. Mississippi*, 394 U.S. at 728-29 (Harland, J., concurring).

tions. In the case of *United States v. Wade*, Justice Brennan, speaking for the majority, expressly stated that compelling the accused merely to exhibit his person for observation by a prosecutor's witness prior to trial "involves no compulsion of the accused to give evidence having 'testimonial significance.'"[6] The courts, including the Supreme Court in the *Schmerber* case cited earlier, have been consistent in holding that the mere viewing of a suspect under arrest by an eyewitness does not violate this constitutional privilege because the prisoner is not required to be an unwilling witness against himself. There is clearly a distinction between bodily view and requiring an accused to give oral testimony against himself or to communicate ideas.

§8.4   Lineup – right to counsel challenge

The right to counsel challenge is not so easily disposed of. In a decision in which the members of the Supreme Court had little consensus, the post-indictment lineup was determined to be a critical stage of the proceeding if the in-court identification of the accused could be jeopardized. The reasoning is that if the lineup, or other confrontation procedure followed by the police, is such as to suggest that a suspect is the one who committed the crime, there is a serious danger of misidentification at the trial.[7]

Contrary to some opinions expressed following the *Wade* case, the United States Supreme Court did not require counsel at all lineups and did not hold that the in-court identification would be disallowed. The Supreme Court referred the case back to the lower court in order to give the prosecution an opportunity to establish by clear and convincing evidence that the in-court identification was based on crime scene observation of the suspect uninfluenced by the lineup. To state this differently, the police can hold as many lineups or other confrontations as they desire, but if the person who is observing the lineup is to be called upon to identify the suspect at the trial the suspect should have an opportunity to have counsel. Even here, however, failure to have counsel at the post-indictment lineup does not necessarily contaminate the in-court identification. It could, however, force the prosecution to show that the in-court identification was not influenced by a lineup without counsel.

The holding in the *Wade* case left many questions unanswered. In *Wade*, the lineup was conducted *after* the indictment. Soon after that case was decided, the question arose as to whether the same rule would apply to a police

---

[6]   388 U.S. 218, 18 L.Ed.2d 1149, 87 S.Ct. 1926 (1967).

[7]   *United States v. Wade*, 388 U.S. 218, 18 L.Ed.2d 1149, 87 S.Ct. 1926 (1967).

station showup which took place before the defendant had been indicted, or otherwise formally charged, with any criminal offense. This question was considered by the Supreme Court in the case of *Kirby v. Illinois*.[8]

Disallowing the right to counsel claim, the *Kirby* Court refused to extend the right to counsel protection of the Sixth Amendment to a pre-indictment identification such as the one in issue in that case. In that decision, Mr. Justice Stewart, speaking for the majority, announced that:

> The initiation of judicial criminal proceedings is far from a mere formalism. It is the starting point of our whole system of adversary criminal justice. For it is only then that the government has committed itself to prosecute, and only then that the adverse positions of government and defendant have solidified....It is this point, therefore, that marks the commencement of the "criminal prosecutions" to which alone the explicit guarantees of the Sixth Amendment arc applicable.

Based on the reasoning of this case, counsel is generally not required at the scene of arrest, where the officer is merely trying to determine if he has the right suspect. But the arresting officer must recognize that even though counsel may not be required in the case of a pre-indictment confrontation or street confrontation, the in-court identification may still be contaminated if the procedure is so suggestive as to violate the due process provisions of the Constitution.

Although the federal court decisions have made a distinction between the right to counsel at the identification process before the formal proceedings have been initiated, some states have failed to make that distinction. For example, in California, Alaska and Michigan, the courts have declared that a criminal suspect has the right to counsel at a lineup or showup occurring before formal proceedings have been initiated as well as after formal proceedings have been initiated.[9]

§8.5   Lineup – due process challenge

If the lineup, showup, or other confrontation is so unnecessarily suggestive as to be conducive to irreparable mistaken identification, the procedure violates due process. For example, if a suspect is in a six-person lineup with

---

[8]   406 U.S. 682, 32 L.Ed.2d 411, 92 S.Ct. 1877 (1972).

[9]   *People v. Bustamante*, 634 P.2d 727 (1981); *Blue v. State*, 558 P.2d 636 (1977); *People v. Jackson*, 217 N.W.2d (1979).

five other persons of a different race, this would certainly make the procedure unfair and the in-court identification unconstitutional.

One reason the Supreme Court and other courts have taken a close look at lineups and other confrontations is because in many instances the rights of individuals have been abused. This is exemplified by the procedures which were followed in the case of *Foster v. California*.[10] In that case, a witness to an armed robbery was called to the police station to view a lineup. In the lineup were three men, including the petitioner. The petitioner was 6 feet in height while the other two men in the lineup were about 5'6" tall. Also, only the petitioner wore a leather jacket which was similar to one the witness said he saw on the robber. At the first lineup, the witness could not positively identify the robber and was called to view a second lineup. At the second lineup, there were five men in the lineup, but the petitioner was the only person in the second lineup who had appeared in the first lineup. This time the witness was convinced that the petitioner was the man he saw at the scene of the robbery. The Supreme Court in reversing the conviction condemned this procedure as a violation of the due process clause of the Fourteenth Amendment.

To be constitutional, a lineup or other confrontation for identification must not be suggestive. If the makeup of the lineup, or the action of the officer at the lineup, is such that the witness would be influenced in determining the identity of the suspect, the in-court identification will be contaminated and disallowed. On the other hand, if it is clear that a victim positively identified the defendant as a result of observations made at the scene rather than at the showup, the in-court identification will be allowed.[11]

Four members of the Supreme Court in a 1972 case explained that the primary evil to be avoided is the very substantial likelihood of irreparable misidentification. Five factors were listed to be considered in evaluation of the likelihood of misidentification:

1. the witness' opportunity to view the criminal during the crime
2. the witness' degree of attention
3. the accuracy of the witness' prior description of the criminal
4. the level of certainty demonstrated by the witness at the confrontation
5. the length of time between the crime and the confrontation

---

[10]   394 U.S. 440, 22 L.Ed.2d 402, 89 S.Ct. 1127 (1969).

[11]   *Neil v. Biggers*, 409 U.S. 188, 34 L.Ed.2d 401, 93 S.Ct. 375 (1972). *Ortega v. State*, 628 SW(2d) 539 Texas (1982).

It is obvious that much controversy can be avoided if care is taken to conduct the showup, lineup, or other confrontation in such a way that there will be no possibility of unfairness or unreliability. If the lineup or showup is conducted in such a way that the witness will be likely to identify the wrong person, the court may find this procedure violates the due process provisions of the Constitution and refuse to allow the witness to identify the defendant in court. This, of course, could destroy the prosecution's case.

§8.6   Pre-trial photographic identification

One method of identifying or eliminating suspects is the use of mug shots or photographs. This procedure is closely related to the lineup, or person confrontation identification procedure, and is challenged on the same grounds.

As the accused is required to do nothing whatsoever, certainly not to give information of a testimonial or communicative nature, the self-incrimination challenge has no merit. Also, as the suspect is not expected to appear in person, he has little claim of being denied the right to counsel as required by the Sixth Amendment. On the other hand, the defendant may claim in court that the identification made at the time of the trial was contaminated by the suggestive photographic identification.

In the case of *Simmons v. United States*, snapshots of the suspect had been shown to five bank employees who had witnessed a bank robbery, and each witness identified Simmons as one of the robbers.[12] The Court refused to prohibit the employment of this technique but indicated that each case must be decided on its own merits. The Court cautioned that the witness identification at trial, following a pre-trial identification by photographs, will be set aside if the photographic identification procedure was so impermissibly suggestive as to give rise to a very substantial likelihood of irreparable misidentification.

It is preferable to make use of multiple photographs of persons who are reasonably alike in appearance. The use of a single photograph was held in a United States Circuit Court of Appeals case to be suggestive and a denial of due process.[13] This is not to say that in all instances the use of a single photograph will make in-court identification impermissible, as each case is determined by its own facts. However, care should be taken to establish identification procedures to avoid successful challenge of the process used. The

---

[12]   390 U.S. 377, 19 L.Ed.2d 1247, 88 S.Ct. 967 (1968).

[13]   *Workman v. Cardwell*, 471 F.2d 909 (6th Cir. 1972). *United States v. Crews* 445 U.S. 463, 63 L.Ed.(2d) 537, 100 S.Ct. 1244 (1980).

key test is, is the pre-trial procedure so impermissibly suggestive as to give rise to a very substantial likelihood of an irreparable misidentification in court?

§8.7   Dental examination

Another means of identification, although certainly more rare than fingerprinting, is the dental examination. In a Pennsylvania case, the prosecution sought to admit evidence of a dental examination to prove that the defendant had a missing tooth in the area of his mouth pinpointed by one of the witnesses. Applying the *Schmerber* reasoning, the United States District Court for Eastern Pennsylvania concluded that the self-incrimination protection was not violated when the suspect was required to have a dental examination.[14] Nor was this a violation of the Fourth Amendment or the due process protection under the facts of the case. The court explained that the compelled display of identifiable, physical characteristics infringes on no interest protected by the privilege against compulsory self-incrimination.

§8.8   Voice exemplars

Many courts now accept spectrograph evidence to prove identity in criminal cases. The constitutional question is whether compulsion to produce voice exemplars for such comparison violates the Fifth Amendment privilege against self-incrimination. This was the issue before the Supreme Court in 1973 in the case of *United States v. Dionisio*.[15] Here, the grand jury subpoenaed about twenty persons, including the respondent, to give voice exemplars for identification purposes. The respondent refused to comply, claiming that this violated his Fifth and Fourteenth Amendment rights. The Supreme Court, however, approved the compelled production of voice exemplars, agreeing that since they were to be used for identification purposes and not for the testimonial or communicative content, this procedure did not violate the Fifth Amendment.

---

[14]   *United States v. Holland*, 378 F.Supp. 144 (E.D. Pa. 1974).
[15]   410 U.S. 1, 35 L.Ed.2d 67, 93 S.Ct. 964 (1973).

§8.9   Footprint comparison and other body examinations

In a minority of the earlier cases, some courts prohibited the use of footprint comparison evidence if the suspect had been forced to place his foot in the print. This, according to these courts, required the suspect to take some active part, thereby incriminating himself. Since the *Schmerber* holding, this is no longer considered a violation of the Fifth Amendment, as there is no testimony or communication.

Nor is it a violation of the self-incrimination provisions to examine a suspect's body for traces of blood,[16] or to take penis scrapings and saliva samples from a suspect.[17]

Applying the *Schmerber* rationale, it is very doubtful if taking hair samples, fingernail scrapings, or other evidence from the body will be considered a violation of the self-incrimination provisions. There is a possibility that a Fourth Amendment challenge might stand if the person from whom this evidence is taken is not legally arrested or if there is no court order justifying this seizure.

§8.10   Summary

Fingerprinting, photographing, lineups, dental examinations and use of evidence from the body of an accused have all been challenged under one or more of four constitutional provisions. These types of investigative procedure has been challenged as violating the Fourth Amendment unreasonable search provisions, the Fifth Amendment self-incrimination provisions, the Sixth Amendment right to counsel provisions or the Fourteenth Amendment due process provisions.

Fingerprinting and photographing suspects for identification purposes do not violate self-incrimination provisions, nor Fourth Amendment provisions, if there is a legal arrest.

Although the lineup and showup are challenged under the self-incrimination, right to counsel, and due process provisions, only the latter two challenges have had any success. The accused should be permitted to have counsel at the post-indictment lineup proceedings. If counsel is not present and this right is not properly waived, the burden is on the prosecution to show that the procedure at the lineup did not influence the in-court identification. Counsel is generally not required at the pre-indictment confrontation for identification.

---

[16]   *McFarland v. United States*, 150 F.2d 593 (D.C. Cir. 1945).

[17]   *Brent v. White*, 276 F.Supp. 386 (E.D.La. 1967).

If the lineup or other confrontation is so suggestive as to cause a very substantial likelihood of irreparable misidentification at the trial, that in-court identification will probably be successfully challenged as violating the due process clauses.

Pre-trial photographic identification procedures may also be condemned if they are so suggestive as to cause the witness to misidentify the accused at the trial.

The courts have been almost unanimous in holding that a dental exami-nation and reasonable examination of the body for evidence do not violate the Fifth Amendment nor the Fourth Amendment.

Appendix

Bill of Rights
(First Ten Amendments)
and
Fourteenth Amendment

ARTICLES IN ADDITION TO, AND AMENDMENT OF, THE CONSTITUTION OF THE UNITED STATES OF AMERICA, PROPOSED BY CONGRESS, AND RATIFIED BY THE LEGISLATURES OF THE SEVERAL STATES, PURSUANT TO THE FIFTH ARTICLE OF THE ORIGINAL CONSTITUTION.

(The first 10 Amendments were ratified December 15, 1791, and form what is known as the "Bill of Rights.")

Amendment I

Congress shall make no law respecting an establishment of religion, or prohibiting the free exercise thereof; or abridging the freedom of speech, or of the press; or the right of the people peaceably to assemble, and to petition the Government for a redress of grievances.

Amendment II

A well regulated Militia, being necessary to the security of a free State, the right of the people to keep and bear Arms, shall not be infringed.

Amendment III

No Soldier shall, in time of peace be quartered in any house, without the consent of the Owner, nor in time of war, but in a manner to be prescribed by law.

— Amendment IV

The right of the people to be secure in their persons, houses, papers, and effects, against unreasonable searches and seizures, shall not be violated, and no Warrants shall issue, but upon probable cause, supported by Oath or affirmation, and particularly describing the place to be searched, and the persons or things to be seized.

— Amendment V

No person shall be held to answer for a capital, or otherwise infamous crime, unless on a presentment or indictment of a Grand Jury, except in cases arising in the land or naval forces, or in the Militia, when in actual service in time of War or public danger; nor shall any person be subject for the same offence to be twice put in jeopardy of life or limb; nor shall be compelled in any criminal case to be a witness against himself, nor be deprived of life, liberty, or property, without due process of law; nor shall private property be taken for public use, without just compensation.

— Amendment VI

In all criminal prosecutions, the accused shall enjoy the right to a speedy and public trial, by an impartial jury of the State and district wherein the crime shall have been committed, which district shall have been previously ascertained by law, and to be informed of the nature and cause of the accusation; to be confronted with the witnesses against him; to have compulsory process for obtaining Witnesses in his favor, and to have the Assistance of Counsel for his defence.

Amendment VII

In Suits at common law, where the value in controversy shall exceed twenty dollars, the right of trial by jury shall be preserved, and no fact tried by a jury, shall be otherwise reexamined in any Court of the United States, than according to the rules of the common law.

— Amendment VIII

Excessive bail shall not be required, nor excessive fines imposed, nor cruel and unusual punishments inflicted.

Amendment IX

The enumeration in the Constitution, of certain rights, shall not be construed to deny or disparage others retained by the people.

Amendment X

The powers not delegated to the United States by the Constitution, nor prohibited by it to the States, are reserved to the States respectively, or to the people.

— Amendment XIV
(Ratified July 9, 1868)

SECTION 1. All persons born or naturalized in the United States, and subject to the jurisdiction thereof, are citizens of the United States and of the States wherein they reside. No State shall make or enforce any law which shall abridge the privileges or immunities of citizens of the United States; nor shall any State deprive any person of life, liberty, or property, without due process of law; nor deny to any person within its jurisdiction the equal protection of the laws.

SECTION 2. Representatives shall be appointed among the several States according to their respective numbers, counting the whole number of persons in each State, excluding Indians not taxed. But when the right to vote at any election for the choice of electors for President and Vice President of the United States, Representatives in Congress, the Executive and Judicial officers of a State, or the members of the Legislature thereof, is denied to any of the male inhabitants of such State, being twenty-one years of age, and citizens of the United States, or in any way abridged, except for participation in rebellion, or other crime, the basis of representation therein shall be reduced in the proportion which the number of such male citizens shall bear to the whole number of male citizens twenty-one years of age in such State.

SECTION 3.   No person shall be a Senator or Representative in Congress, or elector of President and Vice President, or hold any office, civil or military, under the United States, or under any State, who having previously taken an oath, as a member of Congress, or as an officer of the United States, or as a member of any State legislature, or as an executive or judicial officer of any State, to support the Constitution of the United States, shall have engaged in insurrection or rebellion against the same, or given aid or comfort to the enemies thereof. But Congress may by a vote of two-thirds of each House, remove such disability.

SECTION 4.   The validity of the public debt of the United States, authorized by law, including debts incurred for payment of pensions and bounties for services in suppressing insurrection or rebellion, shall not be questioned. But neither the United States nor any State shall assume or pay any debt or obligation incurred in aid of insurrection or rebellion against the United States, or any claim for the loss or emancipation of any slave; but all such debts, obligations and claims shall be held illegal and void.

SECTION 5.   The Congress shall have power to enforce, by appropriate legislation, the provisions of this article.

INDEX

References are to section numbers

Adams v. Williams, 3.3

Admissibility
    Of evidence, 1.4, 5.4, 5.5
    Inadmissibility of "confession" evidence, 1.4b
    Of statements, 7.1, 7.9
    "Good faith" exception, 7.9
    Of second confession after inadmissible first confession, 7.10

Arraignment
    Delay in arraignment rule, 7.13

Arrest
    Authority to, 4.2
    Citation and summons, 4.7
    Definition, 4.3a
    Elements, 4.3b
    False arrest, 4.3b(1)
    Following fresh pursuit, 4.8
    Search incidental to, 6.2
    With warrant, 4.4
        execution, 4.4b
    Without warrant, 4.5
        authority to enter home, 4.5c
        felony cases, 4.5a
        misdemeanor cases, 4.5b

Authority to Detain
    Legislation, 3.2
    Terry v. Ohio stop and frisk rationale, 3.3
    Detention of luggage, 3.6

Detention of motorists, 3.5
Detention to check driver's license and registration, 3.8
Duration of detention, 3.7
Off-street situations, 3.4
Stop and Frisk Act, 3.2 (2)
Uniform Arrest Act, 3.2 (1)

Automobile
Search of, 6.3d(5), 6.4
Search of after impoundment, 6.9
Stop and frisk situations, 6.10
Incidental to arrest,

Berkemer v. McCarty, 7.4a

Body
Examination of, 8.9
Evidence from, 8.9

"Bugging"
Seizure of verbal evidence via concealed recorders or microphones, 6.12

Business
Search of pervasively regulated business, 6.11

California v. Prysock, 7.4c

Carroll-Chambers Doctrine, 6.4

Carroll v. United States, 6.4

Chambers v. Maroney, 6.4

Chimel v. California, 6.2c

City of Oklahoma v. Tuttle, 1.3a

Civil Liability, 1.1
Liability of supervisors, administrators and agencies, 1.3
Theories for attaching liability, 1.3b
Vicarious liability (Title 42, United States Code, § 1983), 1.3a

Civil Rights Actions, 1.2

Citation, 4.7

Coercion
    Of statements, 7.2
    Regarding consent to search, 6.3a

Confession
    Admissibility, 7.9
        of second confession after
            inadmissible first confession, 7.10
    Corroboration of, 7.7
    Exclusion of confession as means of
        enforcing the Fourth Amendment, 7.5
    Free and Voluntary Rule, 7.2
    Prior to arraignment, 7.3
    Warning and waiver, 7.4

Constitution
    Federal, 1.1
    State, 2.6

Corroboration
    Of confession, 7.7

Counsel
    Right to, 7.6

Curtilage, 6.7

Custody, 7.4, 7.4a

Delaware v. Prouse, 3.8

Delay in Arraignment Rule, 7.3

Dental Examination, 8.7

Detention
    Legislation on authority to detain, 3.2
    Terry v. Ohio doctrine, 3.3

Off-street situations, 3.4
Motorists, 3.5
Luggage, 3.6
Duration, 3.7
Driver's license and registration check, 3.8

Driver's License
Detention to check, 3.8

Due Process of Law, 2.4
Effects of broadening scope of Fourteenth
Amendment Due Process clause, 2.5
Lineup challenge, 8.5
Photographic identification challenge, 8.6

Edwards v. Arizona Rule, 7.4c

Electronic Surveillance, 5.12

Escobedo v. Illinois Rule, 7.6

Evidence
Admissibility of, 5.11a
Arrest warrant, supporting probable cause for, 4.4a(1)
Arrest without warrant in felony cases, necessary amount of, 4.5a(2)
Confession
inadmissible, 7.3, 7.5, 7.6
voluntary, 7.2,
evidence derived from, 7.8
Exclusionary Rule, 5.3, 5.4, 5.5
exceptions, 5.5a
"Mere evidence," 6.2b(2)
Physical, found at scene, in support of
warrantless felony arrest, 3.5a(3)9e)
"Preponderance of evidence" test, 7.2
Search and seizure of, with search warrant, 5.1 et seq.
Seizure of, incident to lawful arrest, 6.2b(2)
Verbal, seized by microphone or recorder, 6.12

Exclusionary Rule, 5.3
Confessions –
derivative evidence, 7.8

following illegal search or arrest, 7.5
involuntary, 7.2
Definition, 5.3
Exceptions, 5.5a
Extension to all courts, 5.4
Mapp v. Ohio, 5.4
Modification, 5.5
Right to counsel, 1.4c

Felony
Arrest for, without warrant, 4.5a
Definition, 4.5a(1)

Fifth Amendment, 2.3
Confession as violating privilege against self-
incrimination, 7.2 et seq.
Due process of law clause, 2.4
Lineup as self-incrimination, 8.3

Fingerprinting
As illegal search, 8.2
of arrestee, 8.2

Force, Use of
Arrest situation, 4.6
State statutes, 4.6
Model Penal Code, 4.6
Questioning suspects, 7.2
threat of force, 7.2

Foster v. California, 8.5

Fourteenth Amendment
Due process of law clause, 2.5
lineup as violating, 8.5
pre-trial photographic evidence as violating, 8.6
Effects of broadening scope, 2.5

Fourth Amendment, 2.5
Enforcing by exclusion of confession, 7.5
Constitutional provisions against unreasonable search and seizure, 5.3
Judicial interpretation, 5.3 - 5.5

Free and Voluntary Rule, 7.2

Fresh Pursuit, 4.8
    Misdemeanor arrest without warrant, 4.5b(3)

Frisk (*see* Stop and Frisk)

Fruit of Poisonous Tree Doctrine, 7.5

Grand Jury
    Miranda warnings not required 7.9b

Holt v. United States, 8.2

Identification of Suspect
    In-court, 8.4, 8.5
    Misidentification, factors in, 8.5
    Post-indictment lineup, 8.4
    Pre-trial procedures
        body and body substances, examination of, 8.9
        dental exam, 8.7
        fingerprinting, 8.2
        footprints, 8.9
        lineup and challenges to, 8.3 - 8.5
        photographing suspects, 8.2
        photographs, uses of, 8.6
        voice exemplar, 8.8

Illinois v. Gates, 5.7c

Impoundment
    Search of automobile following, 6.9

Inadmissibility (*see* Admissibility)

Individual Rights
    Arrest warrant
        executing officer to show and inform, 4.4b(3)-(4)
        offense to be stated, 4.4a(4)
        person to be particularly described, 4.4a(3)
    Bill of Rights, 2.3, Appendix

Body, examination of, for evidence and
    identification purposes, 8.1 et seq.
Counsel, right to, 8.4
Due process of law, right to, 2.4, 2.5
Lineup, challenge to, 8.3 - 8.5
Search
    consent to warrantless search, 6.3
        proper party, 6.3d
    privilege against unreasonable, 5.3
    standing to challenge illegal, 6.8
State constitutions and laws, 2.6
Self-incrimination, privilege against, 8.3

Informant
    Tips from, supporting warrantless felony arrest, 4.5a(3)(b)
    Undisclosed, source for search warrant application, 5.7c

Interrogation (*see* Questioning)

Inventory Search
    Automobile, 6.9

Jones v. United States, 6.8

Judicial Officer (*see* Magistrate)

Jurisdiction
    Arrest warrant
        to be executed within, 4.4b(2)
        to be issued in name of, 4.4a(6)

Kirby v. Illinois, 8.4

Ker v. California, 4.1

Lamkin v. Brooks, 1.3

License
    Driver's, detention to check, 3.8
    Firearms, sale of, 6.11

Lineup
  Due process challenge to, 8.5
  Self-incrimination challenge, 8.3
  Right to counsel challenge, 8.4
  Post-indictment, 8.4
  Unduly suggestive, 8.5

Magistrate
  Arraignment before, 7.3
  Neutral and detached to issue arrest warrant 4.4a(7)
      search warrant 5.7

Malley v. Briggs, 1.2, 4.4

Mapp v. Ohio, 5.4 (*see also* Exclusionary Rule)

McNabb-Mallory Rule, 7.3

Minor
  Capacity to consent to search, 6.3d(3)

Miranda v. Arizona Rule
  Described, 7.4
  Exceptions, 7.9
  Required, 7.4a, 7.4b
  Not required in search, 6.3a
  Waiver, 7.4c

Misdemeanor
  Arrest without warrant, 4.5b
  Defined, 4.5b(1)

Misidentification of Suspect, 8.5

Moran v. Burbine, 7.6

Motorists (*see* Automobile; Driver's License)

Movable Object
  Search of, 6.4

Movable Vehicles
    Search of, 6.4

Murray v. United States, 5.7c

Nix v. Williams, 1.4c

Oath
    Supporting affidavit for –
        arrest warrant, 4.4a(2)
        search warrant, 5.7d

Offense
    Nature of to be stated on arrest warrant, 4.4a(4)

On Lee v. United States, 6.12

Open Fields Doctrine, 6.7

Open View Doctrine, 6.5

Pat Down (*see* Stop and Frisk)

Payton v. New York, 4.5c

Penn v. Mimms, 6.10

Plain View Doctrine 6.5

Police
    Authority to arrest, 4.2, 4.4, 4.5
        arresting officer's duties, 3.4b(3), 3.4b(4)
    Civil liability, 1.1, 1.2a
        arrest with undue force, 4.6
        false arrest, 4.3b(1)
        illegal search, 6.8
    Criminal liability, 1.2b
        arrest with undue force, 4.6
        illegal search, 6.8
        under Title 18, United States Code, § 242, 1.2b
    Detain, authority to, 3.1

Force
>   use of in arrests, 4.6
>   use of in questioning, 7.2
>   Limits on authority, 2.2
>   Responsibility, 2.1

Pre-trial identification, 8.1

Private Person
>   Questioning by, 7.9c
>   Search by, 6.6

Probable cause
>   Arrest warrant requires, 4,4a(1)
>   Search warrant, necessary for, 5.7c

Questioning, 6.1 et seq.
>   Admissible statements, 7.9
>   non-official questioning, 7.9c
>   public safety exception, 7.9d
>   use for impeachment purposes, 7.9a
>   use at grand jury hearings, 7.9b
>   Admissibility of second confession after
>   inadmissible first confession, 7.10
>   Confession, 7.10
>   Corroboration, 7.7
>   Delay in Arraignment Rule, 7.3
>   Derivative evidence, 7.8
>   Exclusion of confession as means of enforcing
>   the Fourth Amendment, 7.5
>   Force
>   threat of, 7.2
>   use of, 7.2
>   Free and Voluntary Rule, 7.2
>   Right to counsel, 7.6
>   Warning and waiver requirements (*Miranda* Rule), 7.4
>   interpretation of warning and waiver, 7.4c
>   judicial determination of "custody," 7.4b
>   judicial determination of "questioning," 7.4a

Reasonable Grounds (*see also* Probable Cause)
    Arrest without warrant for felony,
        eyewitness or victim's account, 4.5a(3)(f)
        information from other officers, 4.5a(3)(c)
        informer's tip, 3.5a(3)(b)
        past criminal record, 3.5a(3)(d)
        personal observations, 3.5a(3)(a)
        physical evidence found at scene, 3.5a(3)(e)

Right to Counsel
    Escobedo v. Illinois Rule, 7.6
    Lineup as violation of, 8.4
    Sixth Amendment right, waiver of, 7.6
    Exclusionary rule, 1.4c

Search
    Fingerprinting, when illegal, 8.2
    Frisk, for weapons, 6.10
    Incidental to arrest, 6.2
        allowed, reasons, 6.2a
        area of search, 6.2c
            arrestee's clothing, 6.2c(2)
            arrestee's person, 6.2c(1)
            automobile, 6.2c(5)
            premises where arrest made, 6.2c(3), 6.2c(4)
    Requirements
        arrest lawful and in good faith, 6.2b(1)
        articles which can be seized, 6.2b(2)
        time limitations, 6.2b(3)
    Search of person present on premises searched with warrant, 5.9
    "Plain view" doctrine, 6.5
    Seizure without, 6.5
    Waiver of right against unreasonable search
        area limited, 6.3b
        party must have capacity to waive, 6.3d
        voluntariness, 6.3a
        withdrawal of consent, 6.3c
    Without warrant, 6.1 et seq.
        automobile,
            as movable vehicle, 6.4
            following impoundment, 6.9
        business regulated by government, 6.11

movable vehicle or object, 6.4
open fields, 6.7
premises other than house or business, 6.7
private person, by, 6.6
seizure without search, 6.5
standing to challenge, 6.8
With warrant, 5.6 et seq.
advantages of, 5.11
execution of, 5.8
force, only necessary may be used, 5.8c
notice to precede forcible entry, 5.8d
officer executing to be designated in warrant, 5.8a
person on premises but not in warrant, 5.9
property, only that described may be seized, 5.8e
time limitations, 5.8b
Return of warrant, 5.10
constitutional provisions, 5.2
Security personnel, 6.6

Seizure
"Plain view" doctrine; conditions, 6.5
Stop and frisk situation, 6.10
Verbal evidence via electronic device, 6.12
Without search, 6.5
With valid search warrant, 5.6

Self-incrimination
Body and dental exam as violating privilege against, 8.7, 8.9
Fingerprinting of suspect, 8.2
Lineup, 8.3
Photographing of suspect, 8.2
Voice exemplar as violating privilege against, 8.8

Simmons v. United States, 8.6

Sixth Amendment, 2.3
Right to counsel, 2.6
Lineup as violating, 8.4

Spectrograph (*see* Voice Exemplar)

Spinelli v. United States, 4.5a(1)

Standing to Challenge
    Search without warrant, 6.8

Steagald v. United States, 4.4b(5)

Stop and Frisk (*see also* Detention)
    Allowed, reasons, 3.3
    Legislation, 3.2
    Situations where permitted,
        driver's license, 3.8
        motorists, 3.5
        off-street, 3.4
        person on premises searched with a warrant, 5.9
        seizure without warrant, 6.10
        Terry v. Ohio, 3.3

Summons, 4.7

Supreme Court, U.S.
    Decisions, must be considered by states due to
        fourteenth amendment, 2.5
    Minimum constitutional standards, established by, 2.6

Terry v. Ohio, 3.3, 6.10 (*see also* Detention; Stop and Frisk)

Uniform Arrest Act, 3.2(1)

Uniform Fresh Pursuit Act, 4.8

United States v. Biswell, 6.11

United States v. Dionisio, 8.8

United States v. Havens, 5.5a

United States v. Leon, 5.5a

United States v. Place, 6.10

United States v. Robinson, 6.2c(1)

United States v. Ventresca, 4.5a(1), 5.11

United States v. Wade, 8.3

Vehicle, movable (*see also* Automobile)
    Search of, 6.4

Victim
    Account of, to support arrest without warrant, 4.5a(3)(f)

Voice Exemplar (Voice print), 8.8

Waiver
    Miranda warnings, 7.4
    Right to counsel, 7.6
    Search and seizure, consent to, 6.3a

Warrant
    Arrest (*see also* Arrest)
        validity requirements, 4.4a
            "John Doe," 4.4a(3)
            judicial officer, neutral and detached,
                must issue, 4.4a(7)
            jurisdiction, to be issued in name of, 4.4a(6)
            oath or affirmation supporting, 4.4a(2)
            offense to be stated, 4.4a(4)
            officers directed to execute must be stated, 4.4a(5)
            person to be particularly described, 4.4a(3)
            probable cause, supporting, 4.4a(1)
    Arrest without
        felony cases, 4.5a
        misdemeanor cases, 4.5b
    Search
        execution of, 5.8
        person on specified premises, when, 5.9
        return of, 5.10
        validity requirements, 5.7
            informant, undisclosed to support probable cause, 5.7c
            oath must support, 5.7a
            objects, must issue only for authorized, 5.7b
            proper official must issue, 5.7a
            place to be searched must be particularly described, 5.7e

things to be seized must be particularly described, 5.7c
Search without, 6.1 et seq. (*see also* Search; Seizure)

Washington v. Chrisman, 6.5

Weapons
Seizure of, incident to arrest, 6.2b(2), 6.2c
Stop and Frisk Seizure of, 3.3, 6.10

Weeks v. United States, 1.4a

Whiteley v. Warden, 4.5a(3)(c)

Wiretapping, 6.12

Witness
Account of, to support felony arrest warrant, 4.5a(3)(f)

Wolf v. Colorado, 5.4

Wong Sun v. United States Doctrine, 7.5

Ybarra v. Illinois, 5.9